D1549893

Boundaries in Counselling and Psychotherapy

Boundaries in Counselling and Psychotherapy

Marian Davies

BSc (hons), PhD, PGDipCouns, MA

ATHENA PRESS
LONDON

ISBN 1 84401 850 4

ISBN 13-digit 978 1 84401 850 5

First Published 2007 by
ATHENA PRESS
Queen's House, 2 Holly Road
Twickenham TW1 4EG
United Kingdom

Printed for Athena Press

To Robin and my children

Contents

1 INTRODUCTION

1.1 Counselling and Psychotherapy

Counselling and psychotherapy are provided under a variety of different labels[1] and between three hundred to four hundred[2] models of counselling and psychotherapy have been identified.[3] However, it is widely recognised[4] that there are three core approaches: psychodynamic, humanistic (person-centred being the most commonly used form of the humanistic approach), and cognitive-behavioural. Psychodynamic, cognitive-behavioural and humanistic are also referred to as the first, second and third force, respectively. Counselling and psychotherapy is often regarded as taking place between a trained, professional therapist and client over a number of meetings (McLeod, 1993). However, there are several other ways in which therapy can occur; for example, as a couple, as a group, or telephone therapy (McLeod, 1993). This study will be focussed on dyadic face-to-face psychodynamic, cognitive-behavioural and person-centred counselling and psychotherapy.

---

[1] J McLeod, *An Introduction to Counselling*, Maidenhead, Open University Press, 1993.

[2] There has been considerable debate over the difference between counselling and psychotherapy; some would claim that a clear distinction can be made between the two, with psychotherapy representing a deeper, more fundamental or involved process, and others maintain that they are basically doing the same kind of work but are required to use different titles in response to the demands of the agencies who employ them (McLeod, 1993). In this study, therefore, the terms 'counselling' and 'psychotherapy' ('counsellor' and 'psychotherapist') will be used interchangeably to encompass both.

[3] C Feltham, *What is Counselling?*, London, Sage Publications, 1995.

B T Karasu, 'Toward a Clinical Model of Psychotherapy for Depression II: an Integrative and Selective Approach, *American Journal of Psychiatry* 147:3, 1990, pp.269–278.

[4] A Mahrer, *The Integration of Psychotherapies: a Guide for Practising Therapists*, New York, Human Sciences Press, 1989.

1.2 Boundaries in Counselling and Psychotherapy

The concept of 'boundary' was originally used in psychoanalytical psychotherapy in terms of internal psychological functioning – ego, id, and superego[5] – and a formal and inflexible style of therapeutic relating.[6] It has emerged into prominence in the field of counselling and psychotherapy over recent years;[7] but it is complex with many dimensions. Katherine[8] describes a boundary as a limit that promotes integrity and, further, states that boundaries bring order to lives and that, by strengthening them, we gain a clearer sense of ourselves and our relationship to others. Webb[9] shows that, within different theoretical approaches, the term means different things and concludes that the common element to all ideas of the boundary is the concept of 'drawing a line' or using a 'limit line' that may be between, for example, aspects of the self (internal psychological or intrapersonal), self and others (interpersonal), types of relationships (counsellor, friend, parent, etc.) and types of behaviour (what is appropriate behaviour in a particular context). Owen[10] suggests that the term 'boundary' most often refers to the expectation placed on counsellors to behave appropriately. These limits are set by the counsellor's professional body, their training, and professional literature, and explicitly or implicitly define required and disallowed forms of involvement. For example, the *BAC Code of Practice for Counsellors* states that:

> Counsellors are responsible for setting and monitoring boundaries between the counselling relationship and any other kind of relationship, and making this explicit to the client.[11]

---

[5] E Hartmann, 'The Concept of Boundaries in Counselling and Psychotherapy', *British Journal of Guidance and Counselling* 25:2 (1997), pp.147–162.

[6] G Yariv, 'Blurred Edges', *British Journal of Psychotherapy* 6 (1989), pp.103–111.

[7] G Hermansson, 'Boundaries and Boundary Management in Counselling: the Never Ending Story', *British Journal of Guidance and Counselling* 25:2 (1997), pp.133–146.

[8] A Katherine, *Boundaries: Where You End and I Begin*, Illinois, Parkside Publishing, 1991.

[9] S B Webb, 'Training for Maintaining Appropriate Boundaries in Counselling', *British Journal of Guidance and Counselling* 25:2 (1997), pp.175–188.

[10] I R Owen, 'Boundaries in the practice of Humanistic Counselling', *British Journal of Guidance and Counselling* 25:2 (1997), pp.163–174.

[11] BACP, *Ethical Framework for Good Practice in Counselling and Psychotherapy*, Rugby, Warwks., British Association for Counselling and Psychotherapy, 2002, Section 2.2.5.

In terms of interpersonal relationships, Webb argues that boundaries are context-based and operate according to different rules within different relationships:

> Counselling involves a fiduciary relationship: clients entrust themselves to providers; in exchange for this, the latter offer trustworthiness and expertise.
>
> Fiduciary relationships such as counselling require particular care in ethical management and therefore employ codes of ethics to articulate the rules, which govern their boundaries.
>
> (Webb, 1997, p.177)

Ethics have been described as:

1. The philosophical study of the moral value of human conduct and of the rules and principles that aught to govern it, i.e. moral philosophy.

2. A social, religious or civil code of behaviour considered correct, especially of a particular group, profession or individual.

3. The moral fitness of a decision, course of action, etc.[12]

Ethics are therefore concerned with fundamental principles of practice originating from moral philosophy. The ethical principles that have been useful in other professions, such as medicine and law, and that have been taken up by the counselling and psychotherapy profession, are:

- Fidelity – Honouring the trust placed in practitioner.
- Beneficence – A commitment to promoting client's well being.
- Autonomy – Respect for the clients right to be self-governing.
- Non-maleficence – A commitment to avoid harm to the client.
- Justice – The fair and impartial treatment of all clients.

(BAPC, 2002, pp.2–3)

---

[12] P Hanks [ed.], *Collins English Dictionary*, London, Collins, 1979.

These ethical principles are used to develop guidance for good practice by the British Association for Counselling and Psychotherapy (BAPC, 2002). However, Swain[13] suggests that practising within an ethical context involves more than following a pre-defined set of rules but rather involves continuous reflection on both the process and results of counselling. Bond describes the importance of ethics simply and directly:

> Unless counselling is provided on an ethical basis, it ceases to serve any useful purpose.[14]

Boundaries can therefore be identified in terms of how they function through:

- Intrapersonal (internal psychological) relations that can be explored in theories of personality development and origins of disturbances.

- Interpersonal relations that encompasses the forms of communication through verbal and non-verbal behaviour that are used in the practice of counselling.

- The requirements and limits of interpersonal involvement between counsellor and client through an understanding of ethical principles.

In the following chapters, boundaries are identified and explored in terms of how they develop and function in intrapersonal (internal psychological) and interpersonal relations and how this translates into practice in psychodynamic (Section 2), person-centred (Section 3) and cognitive-behavioural (Section 4) counselling, and the final section compares the identified boundaries.

---

[13] J Swain, *The Use of Counselling Skills: a Guide for Therapists*, Oxford, Butterworth-Heinemann, 1995.

[14] T Bond, *Standards and Ethics for Counselling in Action*, London, Sage Publications, 1999, p.28.

2 Psychodynamic Counselling and Psychotherapy

2.1 Background

Freud is widely regarded as being not only one of the founders of modern psychology but also a key influence on Western society in the twentieth century.[15] Many contemporary theories of counselling and psychotherapy have been influenced by psychoanalytic principles and techniques.[16] Psychodynamic counselling involves condensing the psychoanalytic method and is based on Freudian and post-Freudian theories.[17] The main distinctive features of the psychodynamic approach are:

- An assumption that the client's difficulties have their ultimate origins in childhood experiences.

- An assumption that the client may not be consciously aware of the true motives or impulses behind his/her actions.

- The use in counselling and therapy of techniques such as dream analysis, interpretation and transference.

(McLeod, 1993, p.33)

2.2 Theory of Internal Psychological Functioning and Development of Disturbance

Freud suggested a topographic model of the mind that consists of

---

[15] J McLeod [ed.], *An Introduction to Counselling*, second edition, Maidenhead, Open University Press, 1998.
[16] G Corey [ed.], *Theory and Practice of Counselling and Psychotherapy*, sixth edition, Belmont, CA, Brooks/Cole, 2001.
[17] M Jacobs, *Psychodynamic Counselling in Action*, second edition, London, Sage Publications, 1999.

three levels of consciousness on a continuum varying from that which is clear and present to that which we are completely unaware of. As noted in Corey (2001) and Nye,[18] these levels are:

UNCONSCIOUS

Aspects of ourselves i.e. thoughts, feelings and events of which we are unaware. The unconscious cannot be studied directly but clinical evidence of an unconscious includes: dreams (symbolic representations of unconscious needs, wishes and conflicts); slips of the tongue and forgetting, for example, a familiar name; and material derived from free-association techniques. The unconscious accumulates all experiences, memories and repressed material and unconscious processes are considered to be the foundation of all forms of neurotic symptoms and behaviours.

PRECONSCIOUS

Consists of that which is not immediately at the level of awareness but is fairly accessible. For example, many of our ideas and thoughts become available when we concentrate on them, e.g. childhood memories.

CONSCIOUS

Consists of that which is within our immediate awareness.

The human personality was conceived as existing as a closed system of psychic energy within the three levels of consciousness, in the form of three psychological structures: id, ego and superego. These are described below (Corey, 2001; Gray, 2000;[19] Milne, 1999;[20] Nye, 1992):

ID

The id is unconscious and conceived as the original system of personality. At birth a person is all id and the id is the primary source of psychic energy and the seat of instincts. It is ruled by the

---

[18] R D Nye, *Three Psychologies: Perspectives from Freud, Skinner and Rogers*, fourth edition, Belmont, CA, Brooks/Cole, 1992.

[19] A Gray, *An Introduction to theTherapeutic Frame*, Oxford, Brunner-Routledge, 2000.

[20] A Milne, *Counselling*, London, Hodder and Stoughton, 1999.

pleasure principle, aiming to reduce tension, avoid pain and gain pleasure. However, the id also contains all repressed material.

SUPEREGO

Develops from birth and is the conscientious side of the personality. It contains internalised societal and parental rules and taboos. It functions to inhibit the id impulses, to persuade the ego to follow moralistic goals. The superego, as the internalisation of the standards of parents and society, is related to psychological rewards (feelings of pride and self-love) and punishments (feelings of guilt and inferiority). The superego is made up of conscious, preconscious and unconscious aspects.

EGO

Develops from birth in response to interactions with the external world and is ruled by the reality principle. The ego mediates between the needs of the id and the rules set by the superego and can be thought of as the control centre of the personality – releasing, holding back, or sublimating instinctual drives depending on internal and external circumstances. The ego is made up of conscious, preconscious and unconscious aspects.

Anxiety is considered to be a fundamental concept in internal psychological functioning. It develops out of a conflict among the id, ego and superego for control of the personality and can be described as a state of inner tension that provides motivation for action (Corey, 2001). Freud suggested that there are three states of anxiety (Corey, 2001; Gray, 2000; Nye, 1992):

REALITY ANXIETY

This is a fear of danger from the real world. Anxiety may serve as a stimulus to take action to alleviate the danger and reduce anxiety. However, if appropriate action is not taken the anxiety may build up and incapacitate the person. Reality, initially, also serves as a basis for neurotic and moral anxiety because the original learning of what constitutes acceptable feelings and behaviour comes from significant persons (others) in a child's life.

NEUROTIC ANXIETY

This occurs when the id's impulses threaten to control the ego; an individual will be afraid of losing control. However, this fear is often not fully conscious, resulting in a person feeling anxious without really knowing the cause and/or using ego defence mechanisms as a way of avoiding facing the true nature of the anxiety.

MORAL ANXIETY

An anxiety arising from the superego when a person thinks, feels or does something that is in violation of incorporated values. However, as with neurotic anxiety, it may not be fully conscious, resulting in generalised anxiety with ego defence mechanisms operating.

Freudian theory suggests that a strong ego is essential for a healthy personality in order to mediate between the immediate desires of the id and the rules of the superego. A strong ego will only develop if the environmental circumstances of a child are within normal limits (McLeod, 1998). Nye describes the person with a strong ego as:

> Able to cope effectively with a variety of threatening environmental circumstances, has control over instinctual impulses whilst also providing constructive releases, and takes into consideration (without being immobilised) the values and standards that have been learned, to this person anxiety serves a useful signal that some demand, environmental, instinctual or moral, exists and requires attention. Action is then taken, and anxiety is reduced before it reaches a high level.

(Nye, 1992, p.29)

However, when the ego has not had the opportunity to develop effectively and therefore cannot control and respond appropriately to anxiety, the ego uses defence mechanisms that protect the person from feeling the reality of the anxiety. Ego defence mechanisms operate on an unconscious level and they function in order to either deny or distort reality (Corey, 2001). However, they can be used adaptively to protect the ego from being overwhelmed by unbearable anxiety, allowing a person to function in society, but they have the potential to limit or destroy effective functioning if they become a typical way of avoiding facing unpleasant internal or external realities (Corey, 2001; Gray, 2000; Nye, 1992).

A description of ego defence mechanisms is shown in Table 2.1 and illustrates the numerous ways in which a person can deny and distort internal and external reality. Denial, for example, is a widely recognised way in which people seem to choose to ignore what is obvious to others around them, such as in the situation where a husband/partner is clearly close to death but the wife/partner continues to talk about their future and is extremely shocked when death occurs.

Another common occurrence is the ego defence of displacement where anger towards an intimidating person is diverted to a less threatening target. For example, an older sibling becomes angry with his/her mother but 'takes it out' on a younger sibling with verbal and physical abuse.

Table 2.1 Description of some ego defence mechanisms

(Corey, 2001; Gray, 2000; Milne, 1999; Nye, 1992)

DEFENCE MECHANISM	DESCRIPTION
Repression	A fundamental process and the basis of many other ego defences. Unpleasant or undesirable impulses, thoughts, feelings or memories are involuntarily placed and retained in the unconscious. However, this process uses psychic energy and therefore less energy is available for creativity. It is assumed that most of the painful events in the early years of life are repressed.
Denial	A way of distorting what a person thinks, feels or perceives in a situation that would otherwise give rise to overwhelming anxiety. For example, a person may deny a loved one is dead by leaving a room just as it was before the person died, or married persons may unconsciously reject signs that the marriage is in trouble and continue to act as if the relationship is satisfying.

DEFENCE MECHANISM	DESCRIPTION
Reaction formation	An anxiety-provoking impulse, thought or feeling is actively expressed in consciousness by its opposite, for example, love with hate or cruelty with excessive kindness. Recipients of this behaviour may feel uneasy and 'trapped'. People do this (unconsciously) so that they do not have to face the anxiety that would result if they were to face these aspects of themselves.
Projection	A way of denying one's own anxiety-provoking desires and impulses by ascribing them to other people, i.e., 'these cannot be my feelings, thoughts or impulses because they belong to him/her or others'. For example, a man who is sexually attracted to his daughter may claim that it is she who is behaving seductively, thus releasing him from dealing with his own desires. However, in people who have a largely negative self-image, positive aspects of themselves can be ascribed to others, for example, a friend may possess positive qualities that are intensely desired yet the person cannot acknowledge positive aspects of themselves.
Displacement	This is a process of directing energy from a threatening object or person to a 'safer target', e.g. the man who feels intimidated by his boss and cannot deal with it comes home and unloads inappropriate anger onto his wife/partner and children.
Rationalisation	This mechanism involves offering rational explanations for unreasonable and unacceptable behaviour. For example, in child sexual abuse the abuser may claim that he/she is doing the child good by teaching them about sex. It is also used to defend against disappointment and failure. For example, failure in an exam is explained by claiming that 'I didn't really try'.

DEFENCE MECHANISM	DESCRIPTION
Sublimation	This involves diverting sexual or aggressive behaviours into creative behaviours that are usually socially acceptable and sometimes admired. For example, an artist who produces an impressive painting or a successful athlete are both thought to be sublimating sexual and aggressive energy. Freud suggested that the progress of civilisation is a result of sublimation of instinctive impulses that are redirected into creative and productive activities.
Identification	A way of defending against anxiety of low self-esteem. For example, a person may identify themselves with successful causes, organisations or people in the hope that they will be perceived as worthwhile.
Regression	In response to severe stress or extreme challenge, a person may attempt to cope with their anxiety by clinging to immature and inappropriate behaviours. For example, a child who is frightened may retreat to behaviour that previously represented security – a child on his/her first day at school may become weepy and suck their thumb.

Internal psychological processes are evidently complex. In order to aid understanding of the dynamics in the personality, the model in Figure 2.1 shows a possible representation of the internal psychological structures within a person.

The model attempts to illustrate the Freudian hypothesis that the psychological health of the person will be determined by how physical, mental and emotional information flows from the unconscious, preconscious and conscious aspects of the id, ego and superego. It is recognised that the model can only provide a simple outline to an extremely complex process.

Figure 2.1 Model showing a construct of internal psychological processes in psychodynamic theory

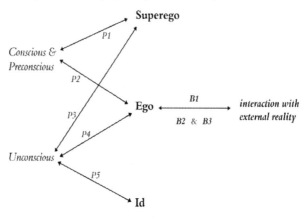

P1–P5 = possible pathways of flow of information

B1–B3 = an example of behaviours that may dominate given pathways in equations 1–3 below

The arrows (P1-P5) show how each aspect of the psyche may interact with the others within the personality to form interactions with external reality as behaviour (B1-B3). The equations below illustrate how particular dominant pathways may give rise to recognised patterns of behaviours:

1. $P1 + P2 + P3 + P4 + P5 = B1$

   The ego is strong enough to access both the id and superego consciously, and mediate between the information received from them. This results in behaviour that is within the normal range.

2. $P1 + P2 + P3 = B2$

   The ego is not strong enough to consciously access the id or receive information from it. This means the ego can become dominated by information from the superego, which may give rise to controlling behaviour towards the self and others. The ego may sometimes be overwhelmed by uncontrollable behaviour derived from unconscious desires and impulses from the id.

3. $P4 + P5 = B3$

   The ego is not strong enough to consciously access the superego or receive information from it. Alternatively, the superego is very underdeveloped. This can mean the ego becomes dominated by information from the id and may give rise to psychopathic behaviour.

It is evident from pathways in the examples above that the number of possibilities, in terms of flow of information within the model shown, may be dynamic, numerous and interconnected. This model provides an indication of the complexity of the internal world in psychodynamic theory and of the range of possible internal processes that may give rise to our interactions with the external world.

The theoretical ways in which the personality develops from birth to adulthood, in psychodynamic theory, has evolved over the last century. Freud initially emphasised development through internal psychological conflicts pertaining to the gratification of basic needs (id psychology) from birth to early childhood (Table 2.2), then Erikson expanded this to include interpersonal relationships (ego psychology), through stages of psychosocial development (Table 2.2) from birth through to adulthood (Corey, 1990).[21] Freud suggested that fixations at any developmental stage could arrest maturity. For example, Nye suggests:

> During psychosexual development, the person may fixate to a greater or lesser extent at various stages. Too much frustration (perhaps because of too little gratification) or too much anxiety about the next step in development (perhaps because of overindulgence) may cause the child's ego to defend itself by 'staying put', resulting in retarded personality growth.

(Nye, 1992, p.32)

---

[21] G Corey [ed.], *Theory and Practice of Counselling and Psychotherapy*, fourth edition, Belmont, CA, Brooks/Cole, 1990.

Table 2.2 Comparison of Freud's psychosexual stages and Erikson's psychosocial stages

(Corey, 1991 pp.103–104)

PERIOD OF LIFE	FREUD	ERIKSON
First Year of Life	Oral Stage	Infancy: Trust vs. Mistrust
	Sucking at mother's breast satisfies need for food and pleasure. Infant needs basic nurturing or, later, feelings of acquisitiveness and greediness may develop. Oral fixations result from deprivation of oral gratification in infancy. Later personality problems can include mistrust of and inability to form intimate relationships.	If significant others provide for basic physical and emotional needs, infant develops a sense of trust. If basic needs are not met, an attitude of mistrust towards the world, especially towards interpersonal relationships, is the result.
Ages 1–3	Anal Stage	Early Childhood: Autonomy vs. Shame and Doubt
	Anal zone becomes of major significance in formation of personality. Main developmental tasks include learning independence, accepting personal power, and learning to express negative feelings such as rage and aggression. Parental discipline, patterns and attitudes have significant consequences for child's later personality development.	A time for developing autonomy. Basic struggle between a sense of self-reliance and sense of self-doubt. Child needs to explore and experiment, to make mistakes, and to test limits. If parents promote dependency, child's autonomy is inhibited and capacity to deal with world successfully is hampered.
Ages 3–6	Phallic Stage	Pre-school age: Initiative vs. Guilt

PERIOD OF LIFE	FREUD	ERIKSON
	Basic conflict centres on unconscious incestuous desires that child develops for parent of opposite sex and that, because of their threatening nature, are repressed. Male phallic stage, known as Oedipus complex, involves mother as love object for boy. Female phallic stage, known as Electra complex, involves girl's strivings for father's love and approval. How parents respond to child's emerging sexuality has an impact on sexual attitudes and feelings the child develops.	Basic task is to achieve a sense of competence and initiative. If children are given freedom to select personally meaningful activities, they tend to develop a positive view of self and follow through with their projects. If they are not allowed to make own decisions, they tend to develop guilt over taking initiative. They then refrain from taking an active stance and allow others to choose for them.
Ages 6–12	Latency Stage	School age: Industry vs. Inferiority
	After the torment of sexual impulses of preceding years, this period is relatively quiescent. Sexual interests are replaced by interests in school, playmates, sports, and a range of new activities. This is a time of socialisation as child turns outward and forms relationships with others.	Child needs to expand understanding of world, continue to develop appropriate sex-role identity, and learn the basic skills required for success. Basic task is to achieve sense of industry, which refers to setting and attaining personal goals. Failure to do so results in a sense of inadequacy.
Ages 12–18	Genital Stage	Adolescence: Identity vs. role confusion

PERIOD OF LIFE	FREUD	ERIKSON
	Old themes of phallic stage are revived. This stage begins with puberty and lasts until death. Despite societal restrictions and taboos, adolescents can deal with sexual energy by investing it in various socially acceptable activities such as forming friendships, engaging in art or in sports, and preparing for a career.	A time of transition between childhood and adulthood. A time for testing limits, for breaking dependent ties, and for establishing a new identity. Major conflicts centre on clarification of self-identity, life goals, and life's meaning. Failure to achieve a sense of identity results in role confusion.
Ages 18–35	Genital Stage continues	Young adulthood: Intimacy vs. Isolation
		Developmental task at this time is to form intimate relationships. Failure to achieve intimacy can lead to alienation and isolation.
Ages 35–60	Genital Stage continues	Middle Age: Generativity vs. Stagnation
		There is a need to go beyond self and family and be involved in helping the next generation. This is a time of adjusting to the discrepancy between one's dreams and one's actual accomplishments. Failure to achieve a sense of productivity often leads to psychological stagnation.
Ages 60+	Genital Stage continues	Later Life: Integrity vs. despair
		If one looks back on life with few regrets and feels personally worthwhile, ego integrity results. Failure to achieve this can lead to feelings of despair, guilt, hopelessness, resentment and self-rejection.

Erikson also used the idea that developmental stages must be successfully completed or disturbance may occur. A summary of Freud's and Erikson's stages of development is shown in Table 2.2 and indicates the possible problems that may arise if conflicts are not resolved successfully.

Freud describes the important needs of a baby in the first year of life as 'oral'. This refers to the pleasure and food gained by 'sucking mother's breast'. If these needs are not adequately satisfied, problems with intimate relationships can occur later in life, due to general mistrust.

Erikson describes the first year of life in terms of having basic physical and emotional needs met by significant others. He states that problems with this can lead to an attitude of mistrust towards the world, especially towards interpersonal relationships.It seems that both Freud and Erikson are describing similar processes but with a different emphasis, from the internal psychological needs (Freud) to interpersonal needs (Erikson). However, Erikson viewed the developmental stages as continuing into old age; for example, in the ages eighteen to thirty-five there is a need to develop intimate relationships, whereas Freud saw development ending at the genital stage at eighteen years.

Klien, Mahler, Winnicott, Fairbairn and others subsequently developed object relations theory, or self psychology, which encompasses interpersonal relationships as they are represented in the mind (McLeod, 1993; Corey, 1991). Mahler[22] suggested that the self develops through four broad stages in the first three years of life as shown in Table 2.3.

An emphasis on how the significant objects/others respond to the needs of the child is suggested to be critical in the first three years of life. If the needs of the child are not met adequately then the child will internalise negative objects or negative representations of relationships, which may result in psychological disturbance through an inability to relate to others intimately and effectively.

Object relations theory can be seen as an evolvement of Freudian instinct theories and is considered to be of more relevance

[22] M S Mahler, 'On Human Symbiosis and the Vicissitudes of Individuation: Infantile Psychosis (1968)' in *An Introduction to Counselling*, edited by J McLeod, Maidenhead, Open University Press, 1993.

Table 2.3 Object relations stages of development

(Corey, 1991; Fonagy and Higgitt[23], 1984; McLeod, 1993)

PERIOD OF LIFE	STAGE
3–8 weeks	Normal Infantile Autism
	Infant unable to differentiate itself from mother. Infant perceives parts: breasts, face, hands, mouth, etc. rather than unified self. When adults show most extreme forms of lack of psychological organisation and sense of self, they may be thought of as revealing fixations at this most primitive infantile stage.
2–8 months	Symbiosis
	Infant begins to recognise caregiver as separate whole object. Infant expects a very high degree of emotional attunement with primary carer. Psychotic disorders are thought to be linked with failure to pass beyond this stage.
4 months–3 years	Separation/Individuation
	Child moves through several sub-phases, away from symbiotic forms of relating to a sense of self-independence from mother. Narcissistic character disorders, problems of self-esteem and borderline personality disorders may develop if a child does not manage to pass through this stage successfully.

in human development (Jacobs, 1999). However, Table 2.4 summarises the central tenets in these theories of child development and shows that the fundamental view shared by these central psychodynamic theories is that, to understand the personality of an adult, it is essential to understand the development of that personality through childhood, particularly with respect to how it has been formed by its family environment (McLeod, 1998).

---

[23] P Fonagy and A Higgitt [eds], *Personality Theory and Clinical Practice*, London, Methuen, 1984.

Table 2.4 Central tenets of theories of child development in psychodynamic therapy

(Atkinson, et al., 1993;[24] Corey, 2001; Fonagy and Higgitt, 1984; Gray, 2000; Hedges, 1983;[25] Jacobs, 1992;[26] McLeod, 1998; Milne, 1999; Nye, 1992)

MAIN THEORISTS	DEVELOPMENTAL THEORY
Freud	Id psychology – Instincts and internal psychological conflicts are fundamental factors in formation of personality which develops in stages from birth to age six to seven. Freud suggested that problems at any stage could arrest (or fixate) development and have a lasting effect on the individual's personality.
Erickson	Ego psychology – Accepts role of internal psychological conflicts but places emphasis on formation of ego through interpersonal relationships as a fundamental process in personality development. The development is described in stages that span birth into adulthood.
Fairburn, Klien, Kohut, Mahler, Winnicott, and others	Object relations – Interpersonal relationships as represented in the internal psychology of the mind. The term 'object' was originally used by Freud to refer to that which satisfies a need, or to the significant person or thing that is the object, or target, of one's feelings or drives. Psychological development, in terms of object relations, is the evolution of the way an individual separates from and differentiate themselves from others. Once self/other patterns are established, it is assumed they influence later interpersonal relationships, matching the patterns established by early experiences. Fairburn rejected Freud's construct of the id, ego and superego and suggested a unitary ego at birth that splits in early life into three parts: the part bound to the object which promises relatedness, the part bound to the object as rejecting, and the central ego.

[24] R L Atkinson, et al., *Introduction to Psychology*, eleventh edition, Orlando, Harcourt Brace College, 1993.

[25] L E Hedges, 'Listening Perspectives in Psychotherapy (1983)' in *Theory and Practice of Counselling and Psychotherapy*, fourth edition, edited by G Corey, Belmont, CA, Brooks/Cole 1990.

[26] M Jacobs, *Sigmund Freud*, London, Sage Publications, 1992.

Although Freud emphasised internal psychological conflicts, these arise from the way in which needs are met by significant others. Erikson emphasises stages in terms of interpersonal development but, again, this is in response to how needs are met by significant others. Object relations suggest that a combination of internal psychological processes and interpersonal relations are important but, once more, this is through needs being met by significant others. The importance of how significant others attend to the needs of babies and children is therefore central in these theories of child development and Winnicott used the phrase 'good enough' to describe parenting that would enable children to develop effectively (Fonagy and Higgitt, 1984). Unfortunately, many people are subjected to childhood experiences that are far from 'good enough' and result in a variety of different patterns of pathology (McLeod, 1993).

2.3 Boundaries in Internal Psychological Functioning of the Personality

The boundaries in internal psychological functioning can be discussed using the model in Figure 2.1 and it shows (arrows P1–P5) that there are indications of internal boundaries between conscious, pre-conscious and unconscious aspects of the id, ego and superego and that the permeability of these boundaries may be dependant on the psychological health of a person. In the equations discussed previously, for example, behaviours are suggested to be the outcome of mental, emotional and physical information taking particular pathways through aspects of the personality. In the model (Figure 2.1), therefore, the boundaries between aspects of the personality may be represented by the arrows P1–P5 and the level of permeability of these boundaries to information between the different aspects of the personality may give rise to the level of psychological health of a person. In terms of application to the practice of psychodynamic counselling, Jacobs suggests that:

> Psychodynamic thought can only be understood if it is recognised that its images and metaphors are ways of attempting to codify experiences and aspects of the personality.

> (Jacobs, 1992, p.12)

This conveys that, although the suggestion of boundaries within the personality may be useful in attempting to understand internal psychological functioning, it is recognised that they are another possible map to guide the discovery of the personality within psychodynamic theory.

2.4 Practice of Psychodynamic Counselling and Psychotherapy

The aim of psychodynamic therapy is to attempt to reveal the unconscious to the conscious for only then can an individual exercise choice (Corey, 2001). For example, Kovel argues that:

> As the unconscious becomes conscious, blind habit is replaced by choice.[27]

Jacobs describes this process by suggesting that successful therapy:

> Enables a person to balance the often conflicting demands of basic psychological (and some physiological) needs; the demands of the conscience (which is not always 'bad'); and the demands of the external reality of the situation: 'an action by the ego is as it should be if it satisfies simultaneously the demands of the id, of the superego and of reality.' (Freud, 1940, pp.377–8)
>
> (Jacobs, 1999, p.11)

Psychodynamic therapy's ultimate goal, therefore, is the achievement of insight into the unconscious dynamics of a person's problems. However, genuine insight is not only an intellectual exercise; when the person understands, he/she will experience a release of the emotional tension associated with the repressed or buried memories.[28] Freud used the term 'catharsis' to describe this emotional release (Jacobs, 1999) and therapy usually proceeds from the client's talk, to catharsis, to insights, to working through unconscious material (Corey, 1991). The basic techniques of psychodynamic therapy are: maintaining the therapeutic

---

[27] J Kovel, 'A Complete Guide to Therapy (1976)' in *Theory and Practice of Counselling and Psychotherapy*, sixth edition, edited by G Corey, Belmont, CA, Brooks/Cole, 2001.

[28] H Maxwell [ed.], *Psychotherapy: an Outline for Trainee Psychiatrists, Medical Students and Practitioners*, Chichester, Whurr Publishers, 1991.

framework, interpretation, free association (or 'saying whatever comes to mind'), identifying and analysing resistances and defences, working with dreams and fantasies, and analysis of transference and counter-transference. These are described below (Corey, 1991; Gray, 2000; Jacobs, 1992 and 1999; Maxwell, 1991; McLoughlin, 1995;[29] McLeod, 1993; Milne, 1999):

MAINTAINING THERAPEUTIC FRAMEWORK

This refers to a whole range of procedural and stylistic factors, such as the therapist's relative anonanimity (rule of neutrality and abstinence), the regularity and consistency of meetings and starting and ending the sessions on time. One of the most powerful features of psychodynamic therapy is that the consistent framework is itself considered to be a therapeutic factor, comparable on an emotional level to the regular feeding of an infant. Most psychodynamic therapy consists of once-weekly sessions, each session lasting between forty-five minutes and an hour (the 'fifty-minute hour' is the psychoanalytic norm and has been adopted by most psychodynamic therapists). However, in cases where clients are extremely distressed, additional sessions may be given to provide support until the crisis passes. Jacobs describes the practice of psychodynamic counselling:

> A counsellor who knows how to maintain boundaries also needs to learn to be flexible, such as knowing when to extend the time if a client is deeply upset at the end of the hour, or sensing when it is appropriate to find time for an extra session, should a crisis in a client's circumstances suggest it is necessary.

> (Jacobs, 1999, p.88)

The total number of sessions can be agreed at the start or left open-ended, depending on the needs of the client and on the way in which the therapist structures their practice. Supervision with a psychodynamically-trained counsellor is recognised as essential for effective practice and an awareness of referral routes for clients, if the counsellor reaches the limits of their skills, is also considered important.

---

[29] B McLoughlin, *Developing Psychodynamic Counselling*, London, Sage Publications, 1995.

In terms of practice, the physical setting of the room should be relatively anonymous to encourage transference and the room should communicate safety and reliability. Communication between therapist and client should not include physical contact because:

1.   Touch can prematurely alleviate pain before the full force of feelings has been expressed thus limiting insight.

2.   Touch, however well meant, can easily be taken as threatening.

3.   Touch can encourage an attachment to the counsellor (whether of a parent-infant or sexual nature) which a client may desperately want, but should never be deliberately fostered.

(Jacobs, 1999, pp.46–7)

The psychodynamic counsellor is described by Milne as:

Adopting a neutral stance based on traditional Freudian psycho-analysis in which 'the rules of neutrality and abstinence' are maintained, meaning the counsellor avoids self-disclosing as this is viewed as an intrusion upon what the client might be trying to reach in themselves and involves a respect for the clients autonomy and an attitude of caring commitment on the part of the counsellor.

(Milne, 1999, pp.145–146)

In essence, the therapeutic framework attempts to provide a safe and reliable 'container' in which the therapeutic work can take place.

INTERPRETATION

This is a fundamental technique in psychodynamic therapy and involves the therapist (in partnership with the client) interpreting the meaning of material brought to the session in the form of free association, dreams and fantasies, resistances and defences, and transference. It is aimed at elucidating unconscious feelings or ideas. The interpretation of client material will also include a client's response to the boundaries of time and space. If a client consistently arrives late, for example, this could be indicating a resistance to discussing painful material or that the client is angry with the counsellor. If a client consistently asks personal questions of the counsellor, for example, this could suggest that the client is trying to undermine the counsellor's role as providing a psychological space for the client to explore painful issues and would be seen as a resistance that would need to be appropriately and sensitively challenged for the therapy to proceed effectively.

FREE ASSOCIATION

This is one of the basic tools used to open doors to the unconscious and, consequently, to repressed material. The intention is to help the client to become aware of unconscious wishes, fantasies, conflicts and motivations by flowing with any feelings or thoughts that come to mind in the therapy session. Therapists listen to their clients' free associations not only in a surface way but also to the hidden meaning ('listening with a third ear'). If a client, for example, talks about feeling angry with his/her boss, the counsellor may interpret this as indicating that the client is unconsciously feeling angry with the counsellor and/or that feelings of anger towards his/her parents need to be explored.

RESISTANCES AND DEFENCES

As the client talks in free association, the therapist may notice that she/he is avoiding, distorting or defending against certain feelings or insights. Freud viewed resistance as an unconscious dynamic that people use to defend against the intolerable anxiety that would arise if they were to become aware of their repressed impulses and feelings. These resistances can be in the form of ego defences described in Table 2.1. Defence mechanisms or processes operate in response to resistances and they need to be recognised as devices that not only defend against anxiety but that also interfere with the ability to accept changes that could lead to a more gratifying life. However, defences can serve a positive purpose by defending people against feelings that are too strong and threaten to overwhelm them or others and so enable her/him to lead a fairly normal life, even if it is a life that in some respects is restricted or impaired. Therefore, therapists need to be cautious when confronting clients' with their resistance. As a general rule, the therapist points out and interprets the most obvious resistances in order to lessen the possibility of clients' rejecting the interpretation and to increase the chance they will begin to look at their resistive behaviour. For example, if a client describes feelings of anger towards authority figures outside the counselling, the counsellor might first gently inquire about feelings of anger towards themselves and then move into looking at anger felt towards the client's parents. This would aim to overcome resistance to acknowledging feelings of anger by approaching the subject gradually.

Dreams and Fantasies

Freud saw the dream as 'the royal road to the unconscious'. During sleep and fantasies, defences are lowered and repressed material surfaces that can give the therapist and client insight into some areas of unresolved problems and an understanding of the client's current functioning.

Transference and Counter-Transference

Transference is a phenomenon that is present in all relationships but in therapy, occurring from client to therapist, it becomes a focus and is used as a means to further understand our deeply held assumptions about close or intimate relationships. These assumptions are thought to be formed during early childhood (as discussed in section 2.2), in the development of relations to significant objects/others, and are largely unconscious and govern much of our behaviour in relationships. They begin to manifest in the client as feelings and fantasies they may have concerning the therapist. Through appropriate interpretations (by client and therapist), and working through feelings, clients are able to change some of their long-standing patterns of behaviour. The expression 'triangle of insight' is used in psychodynamic theory to describe the aim of the transference interpretation. Fig. 2.2 shows that, in the triangle metaphor, there are three points of connection: the present situation (therapist and client); the present situation outside (client and others); and the past (client and past significant/authority figures, usually parents).

Counter-transference refers to the feelings that the therapist experiences towards the client and can be a valuable tool in furthering understanding of the client. However, a distinction has to be made between feelings that are connected to the client's problems and those that are associated with the therapist's past, similar to the triangle of insight. In a sense, the psychodynamic therapist is trained in the art of distinguishing the source of inner feelings and associations. Those that are related to their own past should be dealt with outside the therapy session, through peer support or supervision, or there will be a danger of client abuse. If the therapist, for example, feels unduly attracted to the client, and doesn't examine this outside the session, they may act upon it and use the therapy session to take advantage of the client.

Figure 2.2 The Triangle of Insight

(Jacobs, 1999)

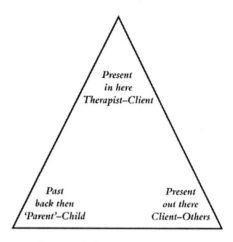

Present in here Therapist–Client

Past back then 'Parent'–Child

Present out there Client–Others

Counter-transference feelings can enhance empathy with and understanding of the client. For example, in a situation where the therapist feels irritation towards the client, if this is examined rather than acted upon, it could provide some insight into how the client evokes this response in other close relationships. If the therapist feels angry when the client is relating their story and the client is not obviously showing this emotion it may be that the client has difficulty acknowledging this aspect of her/his feelings. Counter-transference, therefore, if used consciously, can further understanding of the client's problems by suggesting possibilities that might not be obvious from the client's verbal and non-verbal behaviour.

2.5 Boundaries in Practice

The boundaries in practice have been identified from the previous discussion in terms of counsellor practice and the structures in which the counselling takes place and are summarised in Table 2.5.

Table 2.5 Summary of the boundaries identified in the practice of psychodynamic counselling and psychotherapy

	BOUNDARIES IN PRACTICE
Counsellor practice	Non-verbal communication:
	1. Respect for client autonomy because of 'rule of neutrality'.
	2. Physical contact avoided because of 'rule of abstinence'.
	Verbal interventions:
	1. Predominant focus on unconscious dynamics i.e. interventions largely interpretive rather than reflective.
	2. Interventions with regard to context of the client i.e. awareness of level of resistances.
Structures	Weekly (usually 'fifty-minute hour') sessions with sensitive flexibility.
	Total number of sessions decided with client depending on context, i.e. client needs and/or organisational demands.
	Care taken that structure of physical space for counselling communicates anonymity, safety and reliability.
	Regular supervision essential.
	Ability to recognise when referral of client is necessary.

Boundaries in practice involve intrapersonal (internal psychological) and interpersonal boundaries in terms of, for example, a counsellor's adherence to the rule of neutrality and abstinence by maintaining the focus on the client and endeavouring to be neutral and non-judgemental. The boundaries are also clear in terms of the structures; for example, regularity of sessions, awareness of the significance of physical space and maintenance of professional integrity by having regular supervision and a knowledge of referral possibilities for clients if the limits of a counsellor's training is reached.

The setting of clearly defined boundaries, both explicitly (for example, timing of session) and implicitly (for example, maintaining rule of neutrality) is viewed as the foundation for successful therapeutic outcomes. McLoughlin explains that:

> Everything that happens within a therapeutic relationship is an attempt at communication, whether consciously or unconsciously determined, and this is particularly so in relationship to activities around boundaries.

(McLoughlin, 1995, p.26)

3 Cognitive-behavioural Counselling and Psychotherapy

3.1 Background

The cognitive-behavioural approach evolved out of behavioural psychology of the 1950s and early 1960s and the cognitive therapies of the late 1960s and 1970s (Milne, 1999). The behaviourist approach originated from Watson (early 1900s) and was concerned with objective methods of investigating the influence of the environment on observable behaviour (Fonagy and Higgitt, 1984) and was considered to be a scientific alternative to the subjective area of psychoanalysis (Milne, 1999). It was also considered to be a less time-consuming alternative to psychoanalysis and therefore more attractive economically (McLeod, 1998). The development of cognitive-behavioural counselling (CBC) is shown in Table 3.1 from behaviourism to constructivism.

Initially, the behaviourist model led to development of learning theories (Skinner, Wolpe, Lazarus, and Eysenck), based on classical and operant conditioning, and to the theory that human behaviour is shaped by environmental forces (reinforcement) and is a collection of learned responses to external stimuli.[30] However, there were limitations to this approach and although the development of social-learning theory acknowledged the importance of classical and operant conditioning, it showed that cognitive mediational processes were also important in determining behaviour (McLeod, 1993). For example, in the situation where a child observes his/her father beating his/her mother, what is the cognitive process that influences the child to either repeat the pattern of abuse or to reject it?

The importance of cognitive processes was subsequently recognised, initially by Beck and Ellis, as having a central role in the

---

[30] R D Gross, *Psychology: the Science of Mind and Behaviour*, London, Hodder and Stoughton, 1997.

understanding of and treatment of behavioural problems (Corey, 1991), particularly for disorders such as panic attacks and depression.[31]

Table 3.1 Development of cognitive-behavioural counselling (CBC)

(Allen, 1998;[32] Corey, 2001; Milne, 1999; McLeod, 1998; Salkovskis, 1996[33])

	CENTRAL TENET	EXAMPLES
Behaviourism: Wolpe, Lazarus, Eysenck and Skinner (1930s–1950s)	1. Operant conditioning is explained by positive reinforcement. Responses are strengthened by using a stimulus as a reward. In negative reinforcement, responses are strengthened by removing an unpleasant stimulus.	1. Reinforcements can be food, praise, encouragement, etc. The gradual response is that a particular behaviour ends with a favourable result, which leads to repetition of the behaviour. A behaviour that is ignored will gradually cease as no rein-forcement is occurring.
	2. Classical conditioning is the conditioning that 'one particular event follows another'.	2. E.g. a person who has suffered a car crash may subsequently form an emotional conditioned response by becoming fearful of entering any car and may even become agoraphobic.
Social learning theory: Bandura (1960s–1970s)	Acknowledges importance of classical and operant conditioning, but emphasises role of cognitive mediational processes, i.e. behaviour is influenced by stimulus events, by external reinforcement, but also by cognitive mediational processes.	E.g. if a child observes his/her father beating his/her mother, what is the cognitive process that influences the child to either repeat the pattern of abuse or to reject it?

[31] M J Scott, et al., *Developing Cognitive-behavioural Counselling*, London, Sage Publications, 1995.

[32] N B Allen, 'Cognitive Psychotherapy' in *An Introduction to the Psychotherapies*, edited by S Block, Oxford Medical Publications, 1998.

[33] P M Salkovskis [ed.], *Trends in Cognitive and Behavioural Therapies*, New York, Wiley, 1996.

	CENTRAL TENET	EXAMPLES
CBC (1960s–present) developed primarily through Beck and Ellis	**Ellis:** ABC theory of personality functioning, characterised by 'irrational beliefs'. A = activating event (person's action, attitude or an actual physical event). B = belief about an event. C = emotional and behavioural consequence or reaction of the person.	If a person experiences depression after a divorce, it may not be the divorce itself that causes the depression but the person's beliefs about being a failure, being rejected, and losing a spouse.
	Beck: Cognitive processes govern emotions. Shown through a cognitive distortion model characterised by 'automatic thoughts'.	
	1. Over-generalisation. Tendency to make general assumptions from limited evidence.	1. A car crash victim may assume that every time s/he enters a car, a crash will occur. Leads to anxiety and panic.
	2. Personalisation. Tendency to imagine that events are attributable to his/her action.	2. A person who is ignored when greeting a person may assume they are at fault when the other person was simply preoccupied.
	3. Dichotomous thinking. Tendency to see situations in terms of polar opposites.	3. Tendency to regard people or events as either good or bad.
Constructivist trend in CBC: Mahoney and Meichenbaum (1980s–present)	Underlying principle is that people actively create or construct reality and language ('self-talk') functions as primary means by which a person constructs an understanding of the world.	Gives more emphasis to past development and tends to target deeper core beliefs and is still evolving.

CBC developed primarily from a synthesis of the cognitive therapies of Ellis and Beck. It is still evolving and is currently focussed on constructivist interpretations. The central focus of CBC is to identify individuals' thought patterns and beliefs and how these link with self-defeating behaviours (Milne, 1999). It is orientated towards client action to produce change. CBC has three key features:

- A problem solving, change-focussed approach to working with clients.

- Respect for scientific (logical positive) values.

- Close attention to the cognitive processes through which people monitor and control their behaviour.

(McLeod, 1993, p.63)

3.2 Theory of Internal Psychological Functioning and Development of Disturbance

CBC emphasises bringing about emotional and behavioural change by means of a change in cognitions (Scott, et al., 1995) and is described by Dobson and Block as being based on three propositions:

- Cognitive activity affects behaviour.

- Cognitive activity may be monitored and altered.

- Desired behavioural change is achievable through cognitive change.[34]

It is recognised that significant learning takes place in childhood; for example, that psychological problems originate from 'maladaptive responses or the failure to learn adaptive ones in the first place.' (Gross, 1991, p.102)

However, in adulthood, maladaptive beliefs (also referred to as

---

[34] K S Dobson and L Block, 'Historical and Philosophical Basis of the Cognitive Behaviour Therapies' in *Handbook of Cognitive-behavioural Therapies*, edited by K S Dobson, London, Hutchinson, 1988, p.168.

irrational or distorted beliefs), which give rise to maladaptive responses or self-defeating behaviours, are thought to be actively reinforced by the processes of autosuggestion and self-repetition (Corey, 1991). The focus of CBC, therefore, is to identify the links between cognitions and behaviour and replace self-destructive thoughts with more realistic, rational thoughts resulting in more appropriate adaptive behaviour (Milne, 1999). Beck's cognitive distortion model encapsulates the central defining features of CBC (Allen, 1998) and will be used, in this study, as the main focus for exploring the process of CBC. The main focus of Beck's CBC is on the analysis of cognitive schemata (core beliefs), products (automatic thoughts), and distortions through metacognition. These are described below (Allen, 1998; McLeod, 1998; Milne, 1999; Scott, et al., 1995):

COGNITIVE SCHEMATA/CORE BELIEFS

Information about an individual and their environment is perceived, stored and recalled through schema that are assumed to evolve during repeated experiences, especially during childhood. They are viewed as the 'templates' an individual uses to process information. For example, if a child is subjected to repeated experiences of not being valued, he/she may develop a core schema which means that as an adult events are interpreted to reinforce a negative self-belief, i.e., 'I am worthless'. These schemata are not accessible without considerable introspection and are, therefore, not in immediate awareness. Cognitive distortions and automatic thoughts arise from schemata.

COGNITIVE DISTORTIONS

This term refers to misinterpretations of reality that reinforce negative automatic thoughts. Specific cognitive distortions have been described by Beck;[35] for example, selective abstraction (attending to only negative aspects of a situation) or minimising (down-playing any successes or compliments). They are usually at the edge of awareness.

---

[35] A T Beck, 'Cognitive Therapy and Emotional Disorders (1976)' in *Personality Theory and Clinical Practice*, edited by P Fonagy and A Higgitt, London, Methuen, 1984.

COGNITIVE PRODUCTS/AUTOMATIC THOUGHTS

These are usually transitory verbal and pictorial images that maintain abnormal mood states; for example, cognitive distortions. They are automatic in that they often seem to occur without conscious and deliberate effort but they may be conscious or at the edge of awareness. On analysis, these thoughts may show a specific relationship to the kind of mood states they engender. For example:

> Depression relates to thoughts about loss, defeat, rejection and hopelessness; anxiety to thoughts of threat and danger; and panic to a catastrophic interpretation of bodily symptoms.

> (Allen, 1998, p.174)

METACOGNITION

This is the ability of individuals to reflect, deconstruct and understand their own cognitive processes. This is a process by which adults pass on skills to children; for example, in teaching a child strategies to solve a puzzle, a parent may suggest collecting all the edges, then blocks of similar colours, etc. In CBC, metacognition is the process whereby the counsellor 'shows' the client how to analyse and understand their cognitions and behaviours.

The model in Figure 3.1 has been formulated using Beck's cognitive distortion model, in order to facilitate understanding of internal psychological processes in CBC and, overall, shows how cognitive processes are considered to cause behaviour and feelings. The fundamental assumption that thoughts cause behaviour and feelings is also found in Ellis's ABC theory of personality functioning; for example, the beliefs (B) about an event (A) are assumed to cause the emotional and behavioural consequences (C).[36] However, Safran shows that emotion is being given more attention by CBC, particularly by using techniques that facilitate accessing feelings associated with cognitions through:

> Accessing automatic thoughts in an emotional lively way, or accessing 'hot cognitions'.[37]

---

[36] P Trower, et al., *Cognitive-behavioural Counselling in Action*, London, Sage Publications, 1988.

[37] J D Safran, 'Emotion in Cognitive-behavioural Theory and Treatment' in *Trends in Cognitive and Behavioural Therapies*, New York, Wiley, 1996, p.123.

However, Safran argues that, fundamentally, interventions in the practice of CBC:

> Are grounded within a metatheoretical framework that sees change as resulting from a wilful attempt to modify the self (self-control).

(Safran, 1996, p.123)

Safran (1996) suggests that this may be an important factor contributing to the resistance of cognitive-behavioural theory to accommodate a broader view of the role of emotion in internal psychological processes.

Figure 3.1 Model showing a construct of internal psychological processes in cognitive-behavioural theory

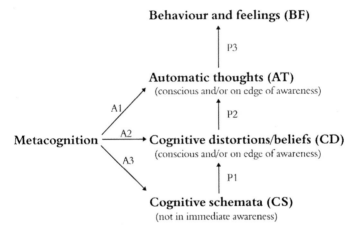

P1–P3 – pathway of cognitions that result in behaviour and feelings (BF)
A1–A3 – pathway of awareness that leads to a change in CS, CD, and AT
depending on level of awareness i.e. whether at level of A1, A2 or A3, and
ultimately produces changes in behaviour and feelings (BF)

In the model, the arrows represent the possible flow of cognitive information in a person; pathways P1–P3 show how cognitive schemata may form the basis of cognitive beliefs and automatic thoughts. In a person who is experiencing an episode of depression, for example, a schema may be that they are worthless, which may give rise to cognitive distortions such as selective abstraction, which is manifest in negative automatic thoughts relating to being rejected. In terms of CBC, the aim is to increase awareness through the process of metacognition, illustrated by arrows A1–A3. The arrows A1–A3 show that awareness can be of automatic thoughts (A1), cognitive distortions (A2), and cognitive schemata (A3). The levels of awareness and ability to change cognitive structures may be related to how the structures were formed; for example, if the core schemata were formed during an abusive childhood, they may be difficult to change and might require long-term therapy (Allen, 1998). Internal psychological functioning in CBC, therefore, is primarily focussed on how thoughts govern behaviour and feelings. However, there is an acknowledgement that cognitive processes can have a number of causes that may require different treatment strategies.

3.3 Boundaries in Internal Psychological Functioning of the Personality

The possible boundaries in internal psychological functioning can be explored using the model in Figure 3.1. The arrows A1–A3 might represent internal boundaries to awareness of cognitive processes; for example, if a person has little conscious awareness of their cognitive processes, then the boundaries A1–A3 might be largely impermeable and a person's behaviour and feelings may be controlled by automatic thoughts, cognitive distortions and negative schemata, resulting in disturbance. Alternatively, if the boundaries to awareness, A1–A3, are permeable, i.e. allowing information on cognitive processes into conscious awareness, a person may be able to challenge distorted cognitive processes and be less likely to be disturbed.

In addition, the levels of cognitive processes that are disturbed may indicate the complexity of problems needing treatment; for example, a person with a fear of flying may simply need to increase their awareness in A1 and A2 (i.e. increase the permeability of these boundaries so that the cognitive distortions underlying the fear can be challenged and changed). However, in cases where a person has been subjected to experiences of child abuse, then core schemata might need to be significantly challenged and changed (Scott, et al., 1995); i.e. an increase in the permeability of boundaries A1, A2 and A3 might need to be achieved for change to take place.

The boundaries in the internal psychological functioning in CBC can be viewed in terms of barriers to levels of awareness of cognitive processes and may be useful in determining the type of intervention needed for successful therapeutic outcomes.

3.4 Practice of Cognitive-behavioural Counselling and Psychotherapy

The practice of cognitive-behavioural counselling involves a stage-by-stage approach that usually includes the following (Allen, 1998; Dobson and Block, 1988; McLeod, 1998; Robins and Hayes, 1993;[38] Trower, et al., 1988; Wills, 1997[39]):

1. Assessment of client suitability for CBC. CBC is not considered suitable for those whose capacity to engage in its logical and empirical procedures is limited; for example, people with extreme interpersonal problems may not have the capacity to maintain a specific problem focus approach.

2. Establishing rapport and creating a working alliance between counsellor and client. The therapist blends empathy with an active and problem-orientated focus and aims to:

    Create an atmosphere where resistance and competition between therapists are reduced by a collaborative, task-orientated alliance.

    (Allen, 1998, p.177)

3. Explaining rationale for treatment. The counsellor aims to give the client an overview of CBC in order to stimulate problem solving in terms of awareness of the role of cognitive processes. This can be more successful if

---

[38] C J Robins and A M Hayes, 'An Appraisal of Cognitive Therapy', *Journal of Consulting and Clinical Psychology* 61 (1993), pp.205–14.

[39] F Wills, 'Cognitive Counselling: a Down-to-earth Approach' in *Contracts and Counselling*, edited by C Sills, London, Sage Publications, 1997.

it is through identifying examples from the client's situation and recasting them in cognitive terms; for example, Wills shows through the dialogue below, with a client who is experiencing depression, how this might start to be achieved:

Therapist: The basic idea of this is that the way we see the world, see what is happening to us, has a big influence on—

Client A: How we feel.

Therapist: Yes. There are probably different ways of seeing things and some seem to help us more than others. If you're depressed, you seem to develop a kind of negative bias...

(Wills, 1997, p.53)

4. Assessing the problem/s by identifying and quantifying the frequency, intensity and appropriateness of problem behaviours and cognitions. An important aspect of CBC is to instil in clients the idea of identifying and prioritising problems needing attention; for example to teach problem-solving techniques.

5. Once the problem/s requiring attention have been identified, then setting goals or targets for change should be undertaken by the client, with guidance from the counsellor, and should be viewed as a contract between client and counsellor. A variety of intervention techniques are used to achieve goals and can include:

- Challenging distorted beliefs. The main tool for this is using Socratic questioning, i.e. using questions to expose inconsistent thinking. For example, in a person who consistently uses selective abstraction in assessing their interpersonal interactions, a cognitive-behavioural counsellor would use questions to encourage their client to be more aware of the objective reality.

- Assertiveness or social skills training. For example, if a client has an inability to communicate effectively in particular situations, then the counsellor might role-play with the client effective examples of communication.

- Systematic desensitisation. The replacement of anxiety or fear responses by a learned relaxation response. The counsellor takes the client through a graded hierarchy of fear-eliciting situations, which can be through role play and visualisations and/or through the counsellor accompanying the client into highly feared situations; for example, taking a person with agoraphobia to a crowded situation.

- Homework assignments. For example, keeping a record of thoughts when feeling depressed in order to expose the negative automatic thoughts maintaining the depression and/or using questionnaires to elicit changes in mood states.

7. Monitoring progress and ongoing assessment. After the initial session/s identifying the problem/s and goals for change, each subsequent session has a consistent structure of reviewing homework tasks, setting an agenda for the session and setting homework tasks.

8. The frequency of sessions is suggested to be once a week, with more frequent sessions during periods of crisis. The length of session is the same as the traditional psychoanalytic hour of fifty minutes.

9. Termination and planned follow-up to reinforce generalisation of gains. It is recognised that termination can be problematic in terms of clients maintaining therapeutic gains. In order to minimise relapse, counsellors need to help prepare clients for ending by exploring how the client will maintain cognitive-behavioural techniques. This can be through role play of worst-case scenarios and by recalling illustrative achievements. In addition, booster sessions can be offered at increasing lengths between sessions; for example moving from monthly through to six monthly.

The length of treatment is agreed at the beginning with the client and is typically weekly for three to four months but can be up to eighteen months if changes to core schemata are needed for a satisfactory resolution of the problem/s (Scott, et al., 1995). Dobson and Block (1988) suggest that CBC has four broad categories of treatments, ranging from brief interventions that address specific fears related to cognitive distortions (for example, fear of flying) to longer-term CBC that addresses core maladaptive schemata that might, for example, be derived from abusive childhoods.

There is, therefore, a recognition of different levels of pathology requiring different interventions and is illustrated in the model in Figure 3.1 with, for example, the fear of flying being in the more superficial areas of awareness A1–A2, and negative childhood patterns of thinking that result from the deeper cognitive schemata as possibly requiring treatment that addresses awareness at pathway A3. However, Milne argues that:

> In a situation where you have events that are very emotionally charged (for example sexual abuse), the use of CBC will not be very helpful because of the need to deal with the associated powerful feeling. CBC methods are most effective when carried out with an awareness of their limitations.
>
> (Milne, 1999, p.188)

3.5 Boundaries in Practice

The boundaries in the practice of CBC can be identified and explored from the previous discussion (section 3.4) and are summarised in Table 3.1. The counsellor practice in Table 3.1 shows that references to boundaries expressed through non-verbal behaviour were not found in the studied literature. However, Allen (1998) refers to developing a rapport with the client, which might suggest that having an open and non-threatening body language would be desirable. The boundaries in verbal interventions are maintained in practice by focussing on interpreting problems in terms of thoughts and behaviours and eliciting change through a task-orientated approach. The structures of practice have explicit boundaries in terms of frequency of sessions and having the structure of each session formulated by agenda setting. Trower, et al. summarise the function of boundaries in CBC by suggesting that:

> The boundary conditions ensure a framework of objectivity and ensure the counsellor stays on the periphery of the client's actual life

... and must involve the negotiation with the client of the number of sessions, agenda for sessions, and the principle of a contract.

(Trower, et al., 1988, p.36)

Table 3.1 Summary of the boundaries identified in the practice of CBC

	BOUNDARIES IN PRACTICE
Counsellor practice	Non-verbal communication: The studied literature had no direct references to non-verbal behaviour but some refer to developing a rapport with the client, which might suggest that having an open and non-threatening body language would be desirable. Verbal interventions: 1. Interventions are directive and focussed on eliciting understanding and changing cognitive-behavioural processes. 2. Contracts on goals for change are made with client and each session is structured by setting an agenda.
Structures	Frequency of sessions weekly (usually 'fifty-minute hour') but can be flexible at times of crisis and counsellor will, if necessary, use sessions to accompany client to feared situations. Length of treatment to be agreed with client at start of counselling. Referral of client when limitations are recognised.

The boundaries in the practice of CBC have been shown to be explicitly defined in terms of maintaining a problem-focussed objective approach. However, Allen acknowledges a structural boundary of practice by suggesting that:

Some patients may be better served by another approach altogether; indeed, cognitive-behavioural counsellors need to recognise their limits and refer patients on appropriately.

(Allen, 1998, p.184)

49

4 Person-centred Counselling and Psychotherapy

4.1 Background

Person-centred counselling is the most widely used form of humanistic psychology. It consists of a broad set of theories and models connected by shared values and philosophical assumptions (McLeod, 1998), and was undoubtedly a reaction to the reductionism and determinism of the psychoanalytic and behavioural schools (Fonagy and Higgitt, 1984; Gray, 2000). A common theme in all humanistic approaches is an emphasis on the here–and–now experiencing of the client (McLeod, 1998). Person-centred (also known as client-centred, Rogerian) counselling has its origins in the work of Dr Carl Rogers (the 1930s and 1940s), an American psychologist and therapist.[40] Rogers' way of working is often referred to as 'non-directive', which emphasises that the counsellor's task is to enable the client to make contact with his/her own resources, and places central importance on the phenomenological world of the client (Mearns and Thorne, 1999).

4.2 Theory of Internal Psychological Functioning and Development of Disturbance

Rogers' theory of personality, known as 'self theory', has central constructs of the organismic self and the self-concept. The organismic self describes the part of the personality that is present at birth and is in contact with the central needs of the person to maintain well being (the actualising tendency). The self-concept is a person's conceptual construction of him/herself that develops from birth and is described by Rogers:

---

[40] D Mearns and B Thorn, *Person-centred Counselling in Action*, second edition, London, Sage Publications, 1999.

As a result of interaction with the environment, and particularly as a result of evaluational interaction with others, the structure of the self is formed.[41]

The organismic valuing process is the term Rogers used to describe interaction between the organismic self and self-concept. This results in experiences that maintain and enhance the organism (actualising tendency) being preferred; experiences that do not actualise the organism are rejected (Nye, 1992). In terms of a baby, this would be accepting food when hungry but rejecting it when full; in adult terms, this may translate into having a clear idea of how you feel as opposed to being confused about what you feel. However, the need for positive regard (love and acceptance) is considered to be innate by Rogers so that if the organismic self is consistently undervalued or rejected by significant others, then confusion about our feelings and needs arise. This can lead to disturbance because of a disjunction between feelings and the capacity for accurate awareness and symbolisation of these feelings, which is described by Rogers as a state of incongruency (McLeod, 1998) leading to inauthenticity. Table 4.1 shows how this process arises in an interaction between a mother and child because the mother denies the internal reality of the child, i.e. the organismic valuing process.

Table 4.1 Early confusion of the organismic valuing process
(Mearns and Thorne, 1999, p.9)

•Child falls over and cuts knee; runs to mother for comfort or assurance.
•Mother: What a silly thing to do! Stop crying and don't be such a baby. It's hardly bleeding.
•Child thinks: It's stupid to fall over; it's wrong to cry. I shouldn't want mummy's support but I need it. But I wanted to cry; I wanted mummy's cuddle. I wasn't stupid. I don't know what to do. Who can I trust? I need mummy's love but I want to cry.

---

[41] C R Rogers, *Client-centred Therapy*, Edinburgh, Constable and Co., 1976, p.498.

Rogers used the term 'conditions of worth' to describe the way in which significant others can influence the way we feel about ourselves through the fact that a child's 'worth' will be dependent on whether s/he measures up to particular conditions.[42] In the scenario shown in Table 4.1, the child must prevent himself from crying (expressing his organismic self) to maintain his 'worth' or value to his mother, therefore the organismic valuing process becomes disturbed. However, this does not mean that unacceptable behaviour should not be frowned on but that, for example, in the case of a child hitting another, the behaviour is unacceptable but the person who hits and the desire to hit can be accepted (Nye, 1992), i.e. feelings of anger are acceptable but it is not acceptable to act on that anger in such a fashion. Persistent exposure to 'conditions of worth' through experiences of significant others denying or distorting a child's internal reality may lead to the development of incongruency, due to the self-concept being out of touch with the organismic self. This is essentially the creation of psychological disturbance and is summarised in Table 4.2.

Table 4.2 Creation of disturbance
(Mearns and Thorne, 1988)

Beginning of life: person and organismic self are one (*internal locus of evaluation**).
Organismic self meets hostility, disapproval, rejection or other negative feelings.
Person becomes confused and anxious because need for positive regard is paramount.
Self-concept formed and conditioned by responses experienced by organismic self, which at same time seeks to protect person from future disapproval and hostility. Self-concept and organismic self often in conflict and maintain uneasy communication.
Continuing negativity encountered, self-concept further adjusted. Stronger need to avoid more disapproval. Voice of organismic self becomes fainter.
Self-concept reinforced, increasingly separated from organismic self, which eventually falls silent. Person now locked into inauthenticity and is disturbed.

*italics added

---

[42] D Mearns, *Developing Psychodynamic Counselling*, London, Sage Publications, 1988.

Rogers used the term 'locus of evaluation' to describe the level of functioning of the organismic valuing process; if the self-concept is increasingly separate from the organismic self (end point in Table 4.2) then the locus of control is primarily considered to be external (external locus of evaluation) and the organismic valuing process disturbed, leading to incongruency and disturbance. Rogers explained how this process of external evaluation becomes part of a self-concept that is largely unknown by the person because:

> The values attached to experiences, and values which are part of the self-structure, in some instances are values experienced directly by the organism, and in some instances are **values introjected or taken over from others, but perceived in a distorted fashion, as if they had been experienced directly.**
>
> (Rogers, 1976, p.498)
>
> (Highlight added.)

He further explains that:

> As experiences occur in the life of the individual, they can be denied symbolisation or given distorted symbolisation because the experience is inconsistent with the structure of the self-concept.
>
> (Rogers, 1976, p.503)

Rogers describes this denial or distortion in terms of, for example, an adolescent boy who has been brought up in an environment that prevents the expression of anger:

> [The adolescent] would organically experience the physiological changes which accompany anger, but his conscious self can prevent these experiences from being symbolised and hence consciously perceived or he can symbolise them in some distorted fashion which is consistent with the structure of the self, such as perceiving theses organic sensations as 'a bad headache'.
>
> (Rogers, 1976, p.505)

In cases where the experience is denied any expression Rogers suggests that:

This may be a basis for anxiety that accompanies so many psychological maladjustments.

(Rogers, 1976, p.507)

However, Cooper describes a further aspect of denial. For example, a man who is generally dismissive of emotion but:

> Finds himself sobbing towards the end of a heavy drinking session might dismiss the experience as 'just the drink', i.e. denial of this part of the self, or seek to contain it within a separate part of the self by acknowledging 'part of me is very sad'.[43]

In cases of serious trauma such as child abuse, Warner[44] describes clients creating 'parts' of themselves (i.e. the experience of the abuse) that are completely denied and are dissociated from the self. The dissociation within a person can give rise to symptoms of impulsive or substance-abusing behaviour, reported memory lapses, nightmares, headaches or odd states of consciousness and demeaning or suicidally-orientated voices (Warner, 2000). It could be argued that this is an extension of denial in terms of Rogers description 'consciously preventing the experience from being symbolised' because the dissociated parts are not being con-sciously symbolised but displaced into disturbing feelings and behaviours that are masking the reality of the trauma. This will lead to an organismic valuing process that is disturbed because the self-concept is far from the feelings in the organismic self, leading to a predominantly external locus of evaluation.

It is evident that self theory is complex and multi-dimensional. However, from the understanding generated in this discussion, a summary of internal psychological functioning within person-centred theory of the self is suggested in the model shown in Figure 4.1. This model is an attempt to provide a map to aid understanding of the dynamics of the internal world of a

---

[43] M Cooper, "'If you can't be Jekyll be Hyde": an Existential-Phenomenological Approach to Lived Plurality (1999)' in *person Centred Therapy Today*, edited by D Mearns and B Thorn, London, Sage Publications, 2000.

[44] M Warner, 'Person-Centred Therapy at the Difficult Edge: a Developmentally Based Model of Fragile and Dissociated Process' in *Person-Centred Therapy Today*, edited by D Mearns and B Thorn, London, Sage Publications, 2000.

person. It is recognised that, in representing a multi-dimensional continuous process into a linear model, problems may arise in interpretation. However, used in the context of a framework to aid understanding, it may be valuable.

The arrows represent an internal boundary between aspects of the self and are placed in such a way as to indicate a possible flow of information within the psyche, which can be physical, mental and emotional. The flow of information is shown in terms of what might occur in a healthy (H) and disturbed (D) personality. The self-concept is shown at adulthood but it is also labelled as developing because, although the development is usually more active between birth (1) and adulthood (2), it will also continue to change throughout adulthood, particularly when self-awareness increases through, for example, therapy. The self-concept has aspects that are conscious, semi-conscious and not in conscious awareness. However, these lie on a continuum of awareness from unconscious to consciousness.

Figure 4.1 Model showing a construct of internal psychological processes in person-centred theory

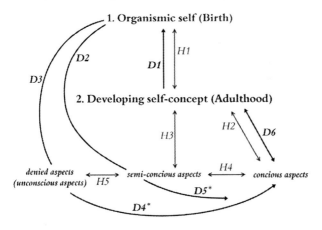

H=possible pathway of information in a healthy personality

D=possible pathway of information in a disturbed personality

*Displaced into mental, emotional and physical disturbance

The semi-conscious aspect may be available to awareness but only in particular situations, for example, in the case described above of the man who sobs when drunk. The aspects of the self that are not conscious or semi-conscious may give rise to a range of mental, emotional and physical symptoms, as shown by Rogers (1976), when describing the displaced anger of an adolescent boy, and Warner (2000), in describing the symptoms associated with people who have experienced trauma during childhood.

4.3 Boundaries in Internal Psychological Functioning of the Personality

The boundaries in internal psychological functioning can be explored using the model shown in Figure 4.1. The arrows indicate where an internal boundary may exist and it is suggested that the permeability of these boundaries to physical, mental and emotional information may affect the psychological health of a person. In a person with disturbance, the arrow D1 shows that the predominant boundary between the self-concept and organismic self may be largely rigid and impermeable, allowing information to flow predominantly one way, from the self-concept to the organismic self. This means that the self-concept is largely defined by introjected values that conflict with the organismic self, the organismic valuing process is disturbed, and the locus of evaluation is largely external. This results in information from the organismic self possibly being directed into denied and semi-conscious aspects through arrows D1 and D2. The information may then become displaced into conscious mental, emotional and physical symptoms associated with psychological disturbance and form part of an inauthentic self-concept through arrow D6.

In a person with little disturbance, the boundary between the self-concept and organismic self (arrow H1) may be semi-permeable, allowing a two-way flow of information to take place, resulting in the predominate flow of information to be through arrows H1–H3 (and to a lesser degree through arrows H4 and H5). This gives a largely internal locus of evaluation and a functional organismic valuing process, leading to few disturbing mental, emotional and physical symptoms. It would seem, therefore, that the psychological health of a person is likely to be determined by the nature of the internal boundary between the self-concept and organismic self, which is developed mainly during childhood in response to the relationship with significant others and to the types of events experienced. Clearly, psychological health can only be measured in terms of a continuum between serious psychological disturbance and complete psychological health and each path (D and H) within the model in Figure 4.1 will co-exist within a person's psyche but, depending on the psychological health, either path D or H will predominate. Rogers described a psychologically healthy person as 'fully functional', explaining that:

> He is able to experience all of his feelings, and is afraid of none of his feelings ... he is a fully-functioning organism and, because of awareness of himself which flows freely in and through his experience, he is a fully functioning person.[45]

The description, 'awareness of himself which flows freely in and through his experience' could be understood, as suggested in this discussion, to mean that in a psychologically healthy person the internal psychological boundaries may be semi-permeable and that denied and semi-conscious aspects are minimal. This is a person with an optimally functioning organismic process, leading to a strong internal locus of evaluation, i.e. a person who acts on their own internal evaluations (in touch with their organismic valuing process), which come from feelings and intuition (gut feelings) resulting in an individual who demonstrates congruency between their inner world of feelings and sensations and expression, evident in words and behaviour (Milne, 1999).

4.4 Practice of Person-centred Counselling and Psychotherapy

The central hypothesis of person-centred therapy is that the person has within him/herself an inherent capacity for and

---

[45] C R Rogers, 'The Concept of the Fully Functioning Person', *Psychotherapy: Theory, Research and Practice* 1:1 (1963), p.18.

tendency towards self-understanding and for constructive change or actualisation.[46] However, the actualising tendency can only be realised given appropriate supportive conditions, which were identified by Rogers as three 'core conditions' and are seen as fundamental elements for effective practice as a therapist. The core conditions are:

- Accurate empathic understanding (an ability to deeply grasp the subjective world of another person).

- Unconditional positive regard (acceptance and caring).

- Congruency (genuineness or realness).

(Corey, 2001, pp.177–8)

The core conditions are described in Table 4.3 and Mearns and Thorne (1999) argue that, although they have been separated for analytical purposes, it is their connectedness that provides the opportunities for healing relationships and that, ultimately, the relationship that the counsellor has with her/himself (i.e. quality of self-awareness), will largely determine the quality of the work that is initiated with clients.

Table 4.3 Description of the core conditions*

CORE CONDITION	DESCRIPTION
Empathy	A continuing process whereby the counsellor lays aside own way of experiencing and perceiving reality, preferring to sense and respond to experiences and perceptions of client.
Unconditional positive regard	The label given to the fundamental attitude of person-centred counsellors towards a client. This attitude deeply values the humanity of a client and this is not deflected by any particular client behaviours. It is manifested in the counsellor's consistent acceptance and enduring warmth towards client.
Congruency	The counsellor's state of being when her outward responses to the client consistently match the inner feelings and sensations she has in relation to the client.

*Descriptions in Mearns and Thorne (1999)

[46] C R Rogers, *A Way of Being*, Boston, MA, Houghton Mifflin, 1980.

A central theme, therefore, of person-centred counselling is the quality of the relationship between the client and counsellor. Fundamentally, people with emotional 'problems in living' have been in relationships in which their experience was denied, defined or discounted by others and what is essentially healing is to be in a relationship in which all aspects of the self are accepted and valued (McLeod, 1999). Rogers[47] identified the characteristics of a relationship that would provide the possibility for healing to occur (Table 4.4) and the practical focus for these conditions is in the non-verbal and verbal responses of the counsellor to his/her client. Corey (2001) listed the 'techniques' in person-centred counselling as listening, accepting, respecting, understanding and responding.

Table 4.4 Necessary and sufficient conditions of therapeutic personality change
(Rogers, 1957, p.95)

Two persons are in psychological contact.
The first, whom we shall term the client, is in a state of incongruence, being vulnerable and anxious.
The second person, whom we shall term the therapist, is congruent or integrated in the relationship.
The therapist experiences unconditional positive regard for the client.
The therapist experiences an empathic understanding of the client's internal frame of reference, and endeavours to communicate this to the client.
The communication to the client of the therapist's empathic understanding and unconditional positive regard is to a minimal extent achieved.

Brink and Farber[48] analysed tapes of dialogue between Rogers and his clients and identified the responses to clients shown in Table 4.5.

---

[47] C R Rogers, 'The Necessary and Sufficient Conditions of Therapeutic Personality Change', *Journal of Consulting Psychology* 21 (1957), pp.95–103.

[48] D C Brink and B A Farber, 'Analysis of Carl Rogers' Therapeutic Interventions (1996)' in *An Introduction to Counselling*, second edition, edited by J McLeod, Maidenhead, Open University Press, 1998.

Table 4.5 The range of verbal and non-verbal responses given to clients by Rogers

(Brink and Faber 1996)

RESPONSES	DESCRIPTION
Providing orientation	Rogers tended to start sessions by giving himself and the client an opportunity to orient themselves to the task.
Affirming attention	Non-verbal acknowledgements.
Checking understanding and restating	By checking that he had correctly understood clients and by mirroring directly what client had said.
Acknowledging client's unstated feelings	Making reference to feelings that are expressed in either non-verbal behaviour or voice quality but not explicitly by client.
Providing reassurance	Either verbally, by touch or responding to a request to hold the client's hand.
Interpreting	On rare occasions, Rogers made interpretations defined as venturing beyond the information given by the client.
Confronting	Sometimes Rogers would confront clients who appeared to be avoiding difficult and painful issues.
Direct questioning.	By asking for particular information to be expanded.
Turning pleas for help back to client	When a client asked for guidance or answers, Rogers would often turn the request back to the person.
Maintaining and breaking silences	Depending on the individual needs of the client.
Self-disclosing	By sharing information about himself with direct relevance to client material.
Accepting correction	When clients indicated that a response was not accurate Rogers would try again to get it right.

Brink and Farber suggested that examining these responses can show how techniques such as reassurance and confrontation can allow the facilitative conditions of empathy, acceptance and congruence to be expressed. It was also found that the types of responses varied considerably between clients, which may have been due to the nature of the locus of evaluation within the client. An implicit aim of person-centred counselling is to help a client internalise his/her locus of evaluation (Mearns, 1995) and re-establish a connection with the organismic valuing process through identifying and rejecting introjections that are damaging to a person's self-worth (Nye, 1992). The greater the proportion of introjections that are not congruent with the feelings of the organismic self, the more the locus of evaluation will be external-ised and the more disturbed the organismic valuing process.

This results in an individual who loses touch with their inter-nal locus of evaluation and has the torment of living their lives by 'people-pleasing' and continually focussing on externally-defined beliefs and attitudes (Milne, 1999). In the case of childhood sexual abuse, for example, the extreme introjections might be that the person feels they have no right to have any feelings, the intro-jected message being that their feelings are worthless. This may give rise to a locus of evaluation that is predominantly external and results in a person being in the position of not being able to trust judgements and feelings about him/herself, which can be a terrifying situation in which the person will grasp hold of even the hint of an evaluation offered by another person (Mearns and Thorne, 1999). A client with such a strong external locus of evaluation would need a counsellor to be extremely careful that their responses (Mearns, 1995) were largely reflective rather than interpretive, because the client will be vulnerable to any externally provided ways of defining him/herself and may internalise inaccurate interpretations.

Responses to client information, therefore, must be viewed with careful regard to the context of the client and provide an emphasis on staying with the phenomenological world of the client. The structures in which the relationship takes place are also an area for expressing person-centred values. Mearns and Thorne (1999) suggest that not only do person-centred values impact on all aspects of the interpersonal relationship but that also the environment in which the counselling takes place should be evaluated in terms of communicating warmth and safety. The format of the sessions will also be structured in agreement with the client, for example:

> It is likely that the weekly session of fifty minutes will be appropriate enough. However the person-centred therapist is willing to extend sessions, increase frequency of sessions, allow telephone contact, engage in home visits and respond to client requests for mild physical contact like a hug.

> (Mearns and Thorne, 1999, p.122)

However, counsellors will need to be aware of the possibility of over-involvement and wider contact should be used cautiously and with close supervision (Mearns, 1995). Supervision is a general requirement of all person-centred counsellors and is normally in the ratio of 1:8 sessions of supervision to counselling sessions (Mearns, 1995). In order to balance the needs of a client with what a counsellor can provide, an awareness and understanding of codes of ethics and good practice guidance is important. Bond (1999) reflects that, unless counselling is provided on an ethical basis, it ceases to serve any useful purpose and the British Association for Counselling and Psychotherapy has recently updated their ethical standards, which include, for example:

> Good quality of care requires competently delivered services that meet the client's needs by practitioners who are appropriately supported and accountable.

> (BACP, 2002)

The practice of person-centred counselling, therefore, emphasises the importance of the quality of intrapersonal and interpersonal relationships and how this quality in relationships is nurtured through genuine, empathic and caring non-verbal and verbal behaviour and through the structures in which the counselling takes place.

4.5 Boundaries in Practice

The boundaries in practice can be identified from the previous discussion (4.4) and are formulated through counsellor practice with clients and the structures in which the counselling takes place. These are summarised in Table 4.6. The boundaries are clearly structured in terms of non-verbal and verbal behaviour in counsellor practice. For example, through an awareness of body language, the counsellor would endeavour to be open and non-threatening and verbal interventions would be largely reflective and non-directive. The boundaries in the context of structures are also clearly defined in terms of, for example, awareness of ethics and understanding of person-centred values.

Table 4.6 Summary of the boundaries identified in the practice of person-centred counselling and psychotherapy

	BOUNDARIES IN PRACTICE
Counsellor practice	Non-verbal communication:
	1. Endeavouring to express person-centred core conditions through awareness of self which includes an understanding of 'body language'.
	2. Mild physical contact acceptable.
	Verbal interventions:
	1. Predominant focus on here and now in clients presenting material, i.e. interventions largely reflective rather than interpretive.
	2. Interventions with regard to context of the client, i.e. awareness of locus of evaluation.
Structures	Contracts are decided with client, e.g. frequency (usually weekly), length (usually fifty-minute hour'), location and type (e.g. face-to face or via telephone) of sessions.
	Care taken that structure of physical space in which counselling takes place communicates person-centred values.
	Awareness, understanding and practice of ethical values that underpin practice.
	Regular supervision undertaken by counsellor.

However, although the boundaries are explicitly defined they also have a degree of flexibility; for example, the frequency, length and location of the sessions are made with regard to client needs but this:

> Is not an excuse for a sloppy, 'anything goes' regime ... but a process of contracting with clients that is disciplined, flexible, creative and respectful.[49]

The description 'disciplined, flexible, creative and respectful' communicates the essence of boundaries in the practice of person-centred counselling in that they are expected to be flexible within a disciplined structure.

---

[49] M Worrall, 'Contracting within the Person-Centred Approach' in *Contracts in Counselling*, edited by C Sills, London, Sage Publications, 1997, p.74.

5   Discussion and Conclusions

In this section, the identified internal psychological boundaries within the personality and the identified boundaries in the practice of the three studied approaches are compared and discussed. The general effectiveness of these approaches are also discussed and explored in the context of boundaries.

5.1 Comparison of Identified Internal Psychological Boundaries within the Personality

In order to compare the identified boundaries in internal psychological processes of the mind in the three core approaches, Figure 5.1 shows the three models of the internal psychological processes that were developed in the present study. A clear similarity between the models is that, to some degree, each approach identifies boundaries in awareness: from that which is not in conscious awareness, to that which is conscious. A comparison of the different approaches to awareness is shown in Table 5.1 and an interesting factor is that, although each approach uses different terminology to identify different aspects of awareness, each theory has three levels of awareness and, for the purposes of comparison, these have been labelled as Levels 1 to 3. Level 1 refers to that which is in awareness and is referred to by the three approaches as 'conscious'; Level 2 is referred to as pre-conscious (psycho-dynamic), 'on edge of awareness' (cognitive-behavioural) and semi-conscious (person-centred); and Level 3 is referred to as unconscious (psychodynamic), 'not in immediate awareness' (cognitive-behavioural) and denied aspects (person-centred).

Figure 5.1 Models showing a construct of internal psychological processes in psychodynamic, cognitive-behavioural (CBC) and person-centred counselling

- Psychodynamic

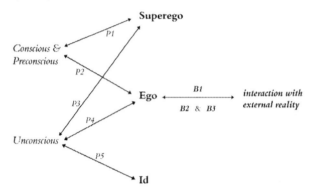

P1–P5 = possible pathways of flow of information

B1–B3 = an example of behaviours that may dominate given pathways in equations 1–3 below

- Cognitive-behavioural

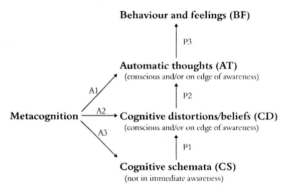

P1–P3 = pathway of cognitions that result in behaviour and feelings (BF)

A1–A3 = pathway of awareness that leads to a change in CS, CD, and AT depending on level of awareness i.e. whether at level of A1, A2 or A3, and ultimately produces changes in behaviour and feelings (BF)

- Person-centred

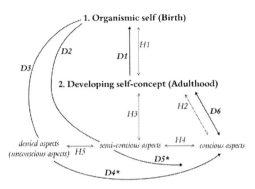

H = possible pathway of information in a healthy personality

D = possible pathway of information in a disturbed personality

*Displaced into mental, emotional and physical disturbance

Table 5.1 Comparison of concepts of levels of awareness in the three core approaches

LEVELS OF AWARENESS	PSYCHODYNAMIC	COGNITIVE-BEHAVIOURAL	PERSON-CENTRED
Level 1 Conscious	Conscious: Aspects of ego and superego.	Conscious: Automatic thoughts. Cognitive beliefs.	Conscious: Self-concept.
Level 2 Pre-conscious/on edge of aware-ness/semi-conscious	Pre-conscious: Aspects of ego and superego.	On edge of awareness: Automatic thought. Cognitive beliefs.	Semi-conscious aspects: Organismic self. Self-concept.
Level 3 Unconscious/not in immediate awareness/denied aspects	Unconscious: Id. Aspects of ego and superego.	Not in immediate awareness: Cognitive schemata.	Denied aspects: Organismic self.

In terms of implications for practice, an important finding of this study is a recognition that, although each approach has different theories of internal psychological processes, each aims to increase a client's awareness of some aspect or construct of themselves; for example, in psychodynamic terms, awareness of the contents of the unconscious is the ultimate aim, in cognitive-behavioural it is cognitive processes, and in person-centred it is the organismic self. This finding can be summarised as:

> **A common aim of the three core approaches is to increase the permeability of the boundaries to conscious awareness of defined aspects of information within internal psychological processes of the personality.**

5.2 Comparison of Identified Boundaries in Practice

In order to compare the identified boundaries in practice, the data generated from the study on boundaries in the three core approaches was analysed quantitatively using content analysis and the results are summarised in Table 5.2. In comparing the boundaries identified, it is evident that the structures in which the counselling takes place are similar; for example, the three approaches all offer usual weekly sessions of fifty minutes with flexibility at times of crisis, the total number of sessions are decided with the client, and all three approaches consider it important for a counsellor to be aware of the limits of their training. However, psychodynamic and person-centred counselling consider the physical setting of the counselling important and that regular supervision is necessary. In terms of practice, all aim to communicate non-judgemental values and focus their interventions on their theoretical model.

Table 5.2 The boundaries identified from content analysis in the practice and structures of the studied three core approaches

	PRACTICE	STRUCTURES
Psychodynamic	Non-verbal behaviour: Non-judgemental. No physical contact. Verbal behaviour: Predominant focus on interpretation unconscious. Interventions sensitive to the context of client.	Weekly sessions of fifty-minute hour with flexibility for times of crisis. Total number decided with client. Care taken in what counselling space communicates. Regular supervision. Recognition of professional limits and routes of referral.
Cognitive-behavioural	Non-verbal behaviour: Non-judgemental. Verbal behaviour: Predominant focus on cognitive processes. Interventions sensitive to the context of the client.	Weekly sessions of fifty-minute hour with flexibility for times of crisis. Total number decided with client. Recognition of professional limits and routes of referral.
Person-Centred	Non-verbal behaviour: Non-judgemental. Mild physical contact acceptable. Verbal behaviour: Predominant focus of reflection of 'here and now'. Interventions sensitive to the context of the client.	Weekly sessions of fifty-minute hour with flexibility for times of crisis. Total number decided with client. Care taken in what counselling space communicates. Regular supervision. Recognition of professional limits and routes of referral.

These similarities might suggest that clearly defined practice and structures are particularly important in facilitating the process of counselling. Hartmann, in a discussion on the concepts of boundaries, supports this finding by suggesting that:

> Though the rules may differ slightly in different forms of therapy, they need to be clear in the therapists mind – through training etc. – from the beginning, and if not clear to the client initially, they need to be clarified – by example and/or explicit statements – early in therapy ... This establishment of solid boundaries around therapy – the establishment of a place in which the client truly feels safe – is a major part of therapy and can require considerable time and effort.

(Hartmann, 1997, p.155)

The formation of clear boundaries in the practice and structures of counselling are therefore important and, in order to provide a general understanding of how boundaries in practice are formulated, the model in Figure 5.2 was devised. The arrows in the model gives an indication of how the dynamic and ongoing flow of information from counsellor practice and training (CPT), structures (S) and the client (C) might contribute to forming the boundaries in the practice of counselling in the three approaches and indicate that it is a process that is not static but occurs throughout the therapeutic process.

Figure 5.2 Model illustrating formation of boundaries in practice

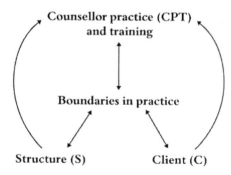

The value of this model is in illustrating how boundaries might be formed and that, ultimately, it is the counsellor's ability to manage them that is important. This is supported in a study on boundaries and boundary management in counselling that suggests:

> It is the counsellor's responsibility to recognise boundary dilemmas and to manage them. Part of the management may be to engage clients directly in helping to define the most appropriate limits ... However, the counsellor is still left with having to make judgements about content focus and linkages.

> (Hermansson, 1997, p.138)

5.3 Boundaries and Effectiveness of Counselling and Psychotherapy

The three studied core approaches generally agree (through different theories) that childhood is usually the source of psychological problems and, in adulthood, the forms of treatment advocated have different focuses, from exploring early issues to staying with present problems of behaviour, cognition and relating to others (McLeod, 1998). Some criticisms of the treatments are that, in psychodynamic therapy, the focus on internal psychological phenomena may obscure other (e.g. interpersonal, environmental) factors and lead to over-reliance on catharsis; behavioural-cognitive emphasis may neglect the whole person, especially the 'affective component' (Karasu, 1990); and a person-centred approach may be too passive and inactive, limiting responses to reflection (Corey, 1991).

In attempting to understand the effectiveness of psychotherapy, research originally studied outcomes, i.e. how much a particular therapy intervention has helped or benefited the client. Studies on the effectiveness of psychoanalysis (in the 1930s and 1940s) suggested that, overall, approximately 67% of the psychoanalytic patients improved, with 33% remaining the same or deteriorating (McLeod, 1993).

However, in 1952, Eysenck published a critique of this early research and showed that studies of people with neurotic problems who had not received therapy, but had been followed up over a period of time, also produced an improvement rate of around 60% but the validity of the results were questioned because of poor methodological design; in particular, subjects were not randomly assigned to treatment or to treatment groups.[50] The main effect of these studies was to encourage researchers to design more adequate studies that resulted in not only more conclusive outcome research but also researched what makes therapy effective (process research) (Barkham, 1994).

In assessing the validity of the process in therapy, Luborsky, et al. (1986) researched the psychodynamic process of transference and developed the use of the core conflictual relationship theme (CCRT). This uses transcripts of entire sessions which are then analysed by psychodynamic therapists in relation to set research questions. Results provided strong evidence to confirm the Freudian assumption that the transference relationship with the therapist is a reflection of the way the client characteristically relates to people in everyday life. In CBC, evidence from process research investigating the treatment of panic attacks has found that combinations or clusters of cognitions are more influential than single cognitions in triggering panic attacks and that the probability of panic is greater when the person has two or more threatening cognitions.[51]

In person-centred therapy, a process of assessing client progress was developed by Rogers using self-statements to identify how the client viewed him/herself before, during and after therapy. This provided some evidence that changes in self-perception are closely associated with successful outcomes (Nye, 1992).

In terms of the process of therapy, evidence has been found that each of the studied approaches have particular aspects which are valid. However, an important issue is which method of therapy is the most effective, i.e. which therapy has the highest level of successful outcomes; this has be extensively researched (Barkham, 1994). The most conclusive evidence is from meta-analysis of secondary data of outcome studies and resulted in the conclusion that, despite the differences:

---

[50] M Barkham, 'Research in Individual Therapy' in *Individual Therapy in Britain Today*, edited by W Dryden, New York, W Harper and Row, 1994.

[51] M Marks et al., 'Are Anxiety Symptoms and Claustrophobic Cognitions Directly Related?', *Journal of Anxiety Disorders* 5 (1991), pp.247–54.

There is little doubt that psychological treatments are, overall and in general, beneficial, although it remains equally true that not everyone benefits to a satisfactory degree.[52]

More recently, Clarkson summarises the results of researcher's attempts to compare effectiveness of therapies:

There is the unremitting inconclusiveness of quantitative empirical evidence attempting to prove that any one theoretical approach is more effective than another across a broad spectrum of problems.[53]

The effectiveness of counselling has, therefore, been established and, in attempting to identify the common factors that give rise to successful outcomes, Sloane, et al.[54] compared the effectiveness of psychodynamic therapy with that of a behavioural approach (over two years) and found that both treatment groups improved more than the waiting list group. They also found that successful clients, irrespective of the therapy they received, identified the personality of the therapist, the provision of understanding of problems, encouragement to face problems and help towards a greater self-understanding as the most important factors in their recovery.

The importance of the therapeutic relationship has also been found in research on the treatment of depression. In a study by Elkin, et al. (cited in Karasu, 1990), it was found that an initial supportive approach (sympathetic attention and encouragement) in the clinical management of depressed patients (with or without pharmacotherapy) before treatment begins, increases the effectiveness of the treatment. In meta-analysis of the results of research comparing the outcomes of different approaches to counselling and psychotherapy, the overall conclusion has been that (Field, 1996;[55] Clarkson, 1998; McLeod, 1998):

---

[52] M J Lambert et al., *The Assessment of Psychotherapy Outcome*, New York, Wiley, 1986, p.158.

[53] P Clarkson, 'Researching the "Therapeutic Relationship" in Psychoanalysis, Counselling Psychology and Psychotherapy. A Qualitative Enquiry' in *Integrating Theory Research and Supervised Practice*, edited by P Clarkson, Chichester, Whurr publishers, 1998, p.74.

[54] R B Sloane et al., 'Short-term Analytical Psychotherapy Versus Behaviour Therapy', *American Journal of Psychiatry* 132 (1975), pp.373–7.

[55] N Field, *Breakdown and Breakthrough*, Oxford, Routledge, 1996.

Psychological healing depends less on adherence to any specific approach and more on the quality of relationship between therapist and client.

Holmes[56] argues that attachment theory, originally from research carried out by Bowlby and Ainsworth, provides a theoretical basis for the research finding that a good therapeutic alliance is the best predictor of good outcome in therapy. Attachment theory suggests that attachment experience of young children, to significant others, becomes internalised as a self-narrative and disturbance of these attachments can be the cause of psychological problems in children and adults (Holmes, 1997). This has been supported by research on the effects of early influences on subsequent behaviour, which showed that infants brought up in institutions that had fast turnovers (some fifty different caretakers and hence no chance for the children to form lasting relationships) continued as children to be more clinging, attention-seeking and disobedient and this pattern persisted even if they had left the institution by the age of four to live in a family.[57]

Rutter, et al.[58] followed up institution-reared children in their mid-twenties and found substantially more psychiatric, criminal and relationship problems in this group than in a sample taken from the general population and that outcome was significantly associated with the quality of caretaking during infancy, early and prolonged experience of multiple caretaking having particularly severe consequences. The research, therefore, suggests that the quality of relationships in early life are vital to healthy psychological development and that, in the therapeutic environment, the quality of the relationship between client and therapist is an essential factor for psychological healing. Could it be that the

---

[56] J Holmes, 'Attachment, Autonomy, Intimacy: some Clinical Implications of Attachment Theory', *British Journal of Medical Psychology* 70 (1997), pp.209–15.

[57] B Tizard and J Hodges, 'The Effect of Early Institutional Rearing on the Development of Eight-year old Children (1978)' in *Personality Theory and Clinical Practice*, edited by P Fonagy and A Higgitt, London, Methuen, 1984.

[58] M Rutter et al., 'Parenting in Two Generations: Looking Backwards and Looking Forwards' in *Personality Theory and Clinical Practice*, edited by P Fonagy and A Higgitt, London, Methuen, 1984.

quality of relationships is a consequence of how the boundaries operate in the relationship and particularly how the 'more powerful' person e.g. parent, significant other or counsellor, manage the boundaries? In terms of interpersonal relationships, Webb supports this hypothesis by suggesting that:

> The relationship between a parent and a child will have different rules from that which the same child has with her/his teacher. Rules are negotiated, although this may not be evident at the time to the parties involved. The more power a person has in the relationship, the more influence they have in the negotiation process and the more responsibility they carry for good management of the boundaries. Rules governing relationship boundaries are in general unexpressed and based largely upon cultural norms and expectations.

(Webb, 1997, p.177)

In determining the possible link between boundary management by the more powerful party in a relationship, the context of boundary violations is important. In the context of boundary violations in relationships, Katherine suggests that:

> Boundaries tell us that certain behaviour is inappropriate in the context of certain relationships. All relationships, even very intimate ones, have limits on what's appropriate. When someone acts inappropriately within the context of the relationship, it often leads to boundary violation.[59]

Katherine explains what constitutes a violation:

> A boundary violation is committed when someone knowingly or unknowingly crosses the emotional, physical, spiritual or sexual limits of another. Boundary violations can be accidental or deliberate. They can be committed maliciously, thoughtlessly or out of kindness; for example, boundary violations of children by adults occurs when the child's needs become subjugated to those of the adult, whether conscious or not.

(Katherine, 2000, p.135)

Hartmann suggests that in the context of the relationship between a client and counsellor that:

---

[59] A Katherine, *Boundaries: Where You End and I Begin*, second edition, Illinois, Parkside Publishing, 2000, p.136.

> A boundary violation occurs whenever the therapist acts on the basis of his or her own needs or desires rather than the client's needs and best interest. This is true unfortunately even when the needs are not entirely conscious.
>
> (Hartmann, 1997, p.155)

In terms of abuse of clients by counsellors, it has been found that a general 'loosening of boundaries' often precedes sexual abuse; for example, Norris et al (2003)[60], in research into psychotherapist-patient sexual abuse, suggests that use of first names, the extension of length of sessions and flexible appointment times are the first three steps on path to full sexual relations. The possibility of boundary violations clearly rests with the most powerful party in the relationship and Webb further supports this by explaining that:

> Counselling involves a fiduciary relationship: clients entrust themselves to providers; in exchange for this, the latter offer trustworthiness and expertise. Clients, however, cannot readily judge the appropriateness of counselling dynamics for themselves and need additional protection. Fiduciary relationships such as counselling require particular care in ethical management and therefore employ codes of ethics to articulate the rules, which govern their boundaries.
>
> (Webb, 1997, p.177)

The conclusion generated from this study, therefore, is:

> The quality of the therapeutic relationship is largely determined by the quality of intrapersonal and interpersonal boundary management practices by the counsellor and psychotherapist and, therefore, boundary management is an important determining factor in achieving successful therapeutic outcomes.

The similarities of different approaches to counselling have also been explored by a qualitative enquiry into the 'therapeutic relationship' in psychoanalysis, counselling psychology and psychotherapy in which Clarkson hypothesised:

---

[60] D M Norris, T G Gutheil and L H Strasburger, 'This Couldn't happen to Me: Boundary Problems and Sexual Misconduct in the Psychotherapy Relationship', *Psychiatric Services* 54 :4 (2003), pp. 517-522

Could it be that these many different approaches are all talking about the therapeutic relationship but from different universes of discourse or focussing on different aspects of it?

(Clarkson, 1998, p.75)

This also suggests that the different theories might be referring to similar processes but through different forms of discourse and provides further evidence of a common element, e.g. boundary management, in the therapies being a major factor in successful therapeutic outcomes. Hermansson, in a study of boundaries and boundary management in counselling, concluded that:

It is imperative that functional boundaries operate; excessive rigidity can bring disfunctionality – an inability to communicate effectively; excessive looseness will also bring disfunctionality – a loss of identity; in all matters of boundary, in counselling as in life, a living, dynamic quality must exist.

(Hermansson, 1997, p.144)

This description conveys the importance of understanding and effectively managing boundaries in any approach to counselling and psychotherapy and further supports the conclusion that effective management of intrapersonal (internal psychological) and interpersonal boundaries by a counsellor and psychotherapist has a significant influence on successful therapeutic outcomes.

6 References

Allen, N B, 'Cognitive Psychotherapy' in *An Introduction to the Psychotherapies*, edited by S Bloch, Oxford Medical Publications, 1998

Atkinson, R L, Atkinson, R C, Smith, E E and Bem, D J, *Introduction to Psychology*, eleventh edition, Orlando, Harcourt Brace College, 1993

BACP, *Ethical Framework for Good Practice in Counselling and Psychotherapy*, Rugby, Warwks., British Association for Counselling and Psychotherapy, 2002

Barkham, M, 'Research in Individual Therapy' in *Individual Therapy in Britain*, edited by W Dryden, New York, W Harper and Row, 1994

Barlow, D H, Hayes, S C and Nelson, R O, *The Scientist-Practitioner: Research and Accountability in Clinical and Educational Settings*, New York, Pergamon, 1984

Beck, A T, 'Cognitive Therapy and Emotional Disorders (1976)' in *Personality Theory and Clinical Practice*, edited by P Fonagy and A Higgitt, London, Methuen, 1984

Bell, C, 'Studying the Locally Powerful: Personal Reflections on a Research Career (1978)' in *Practical Social Research*, edited by D Hall and I Hall, Basingstoke, Macmillan, 1996

Blaikie, N, 'Approaches to Social Enquiry (1993)' in *Practical Social Research*, edited by D Hall and I Hall, Basingstoke, Macmillan, 1996

Bohart, A C, 'Psychotherapy Integration from a Client-centred Perspective' in *Client-centred and Experiential Psychotherapy in the Nineties*, edited by G Lieter, J Rombauts and R Van Balen, Leuvan University Press, 1990

Bond, T, *Standards and Ethics for Counselling in Action*, London, Sage Publications, 1999

Bordin, E S, 'The Generalisability of the Psychoanalytic Concept of Working Alliance', *Psychotherapy: Theory, Research and Practice* 16 (1989), 252–260

Brink, D C and Farber, B A, 'Analysis of Carl Rogers' Therapeutic Interventions (1996)' in *An Introduction to Counselling*, second edition, edited by J McLeod, Maidenhead, Open University Press, 1998

Bryman, A, *Quantity and Quality in Social Research*, Oxford, Routledge, 1995

Cancian, F M, 'Conflicts between Activist Research and Academic Success: Participatory Research and Alternative Strategies', *The American Sociologist* 81 (1993), 92–106

Clarkson, P, 'Researching the "Therapeutic Relationship" in Psychoanalysis, Counselling Psychology and Psychotherapy. A Qualitative Enquiry' in *Integrating Theory, Research and Supervised Practice*, edited by P Clarkson, Chichester, Whurr Publishers, 1998

Cooper, M, '"If you can't be Jekyll be Hyde": an Existential-Phenomenological Approach of Lived Plurality (1999)' in *Person Centred Therapy Today*, edited by D Mearns and B Thorn, London, Sage Publications, 2000

Corey, G [ed.], *Theory and Practice of Counselling and Psychotherapy*, fourth edition, Belmont, CA, Brooks/Cole, 1990

—— [ed.], *Theory and Practice of Counselling and Psychotherapy*, sixth edition, Belmont, CA, Brooks/Cole, 2001

Crits-Christoph, P, Cooper, A and Luborsky, L, '"The Accuracy of Therapists" Interpretations and the Outcome of Dynamic Psychotherapy', *Journal of Consulting and Clinical Psychology* 56 (1988), 490–495

Dobson, K S and Block, L, 'Historical and Philosophical Basis of the Cognitive Behaviour Therapies' in *Handbook of Cognitive-behavioural Therapies*, edited by K S Dobson, London, Hutchinson, 1988

Ellis, A, 'Reason and Emotion in Psychotherapy (1962)' in *An Introduction to Counselling,* edited by J McLeod, Maidenhead, Open University Press, 1993

Feltham, C, *What is Counselling?*, London, Sage Publications, 1995

Field, N, *Breakdown and Breakthrough*, Oxford, Routledge, 1996

Fonagy, P and Higgitt, A [eds], *Personality Theory and Clinical Practice*, London, Methuen, 1984

Gray, A, *An Introduction to the Therapeutic Frame*, Oxford, Brunner-Routledge, 2000

Gross, R D, *Psychology: the Science of Mind and Behaviour*, London, Hodder and Stoughton, 1991

Gross, R, Humphreys, P and Petkova, B, *Challenges in Psychology*, London, Hodder and Stoughton, 1997

Hall, D and Hall, I [eds], *Practical Social Research*, Basingstoke, Macmillan, 1996

Hanks, P [ed.], *Collins English Dictionary*, London, Collins, 1979

Hartmann, E, 'The Concept of Boundaries in Counselling and Psychotherapy', *British Journal of Guidance and Counselling* 25:2 (1997), 147–162

Hedges, L E, 'Listening Perspectives in Psychotherapy (1983)' in *Theory and Practice of Counselling and Psychotherapy*, fourth edition, edited by G Corey, Belmont, CA, Brooks/Cole, 1990

Hermansson, G, 'Boundaries and Boundary Management in Counselling: the Never Ending Story', *British Journal of Guidance and Counselling* 25:2 (1997), 133–146

Hessler, R M, 'Social Research Methods (1992)' in *Practical Social Research,* edited by D Hall and I Hall, London, Macmillan, 1996

Holmes, J, 'Attachment, Autonomy, Intimacy: some Clinical Implications of Attachment Theory', *British Journal of Medical Psychology* 70 (1997), 209–15

House, R, 'An Approach to Time-limited Humanistic-dynamic Counselling', *British Journal of Guidance and Counselling* 25:2 (1997), 251–262

Jacobs, M, *Sigmund Freud*, London, Sage Publications, 1992

——, *Psychodynamic Counselling in Action*, second edition, London, Sage Publications, 1999

Jayaratne, T E, 'The Value of Quantitative Methodology for Feminist Research' in *Social Research: Philosophy, Politics and Practice*, edited by M Hammersley, London, Sage Publications, 1993

Karasu, B T, 'Toward a Clinical Model of Psychotherapy for Depression II: an Integrative and Selective Approach, *American Journal of Psychiatry* 147:3 (1990), 269–278

Katherine, A, *Boundaries: Where You End and I Begin*, Illinois, Parkside Publishing, 1991

——, *Boundaries: Where You End and I Begin*, second edition, Illinois, Parkside Publishing, 2000

Kovel, J, 'A Complete Guide to Therapy (1976)' in *Theory and Practice of Counselling and Psychotherapy*, sixth edition, edited by G Corey, Belmont, CA, Brooks/Cole, 2001

Lambert, M J, Christensen, E R and DeJulio, S S, *The Assessment of Psychotherapy Outcome*, New York, Wiley, 1986

Luborsky, L, Crits-Christoph, P and Mellon, J, 'Advent of Objective Measures of the Transference Concept, *Journal of Consulting and Clinical Psychology* 54: 3 (1986), 9–47

Mahler, M S, 'On Human Symbiosis and the Vicissitudes of Individuation: Infantile Psychosis (1968)' in *An Introduction to Counselling*, edited by J McLeod, Maidenhead, Open University Press, 1993

Mahrer, A, *The Integration of Psychotherapies: a Guide for Practising Therapists*, New York, Human Sciences Press, 1989

Marks, M, Basoglu, M, Alkubaisy, T, Seguia, S and Marks, I M 'Are Anxiety Symptoms and Claustrophobic Cognitions Directly Related?', *Journal of Anxiety Disorders* 5 (1991), 247–254

Mason, J, *Against Therapy*, London, Fontana Press, 1990

Maxwell, H, [ed.], *Psychotherapy: an Outline for Trainee Psychiatrists, Medical Students and Practitioners*, Chichester, Whurr Publishers, 1991

Maynard, M and Purvis, J, 'Doing Feminist Research' in *Researching Women's Lives from a Feminist Perspective,* London, Taylor and Francis, 1994

May, T, *Social Research: Issues, Methods and Process*, second edition, London, Open University Press, 1998

McLeod, J [ed.], *An Introduction to Counselling*, Maidenhead, Open University Press, 1993

—— [ed.], *An Introduction to Counselling*, second edition, Maidenhead, Open University Press, 1998

McLoughlin, B, *Developing Psychodynamic Counselling*, London, Sage Publications, 1995.

Mearns, D, *Developing Person-Centred Counselling*, London, Sage Publications, 1995

Mearns, D and Thorn, B, *Person-Centred Counselling in Action*, London, Sage Publications, 1988

Mearns, D and Thorn, B, *Person-Centred Counselling in Action*, second edition, London, Sage Publications, 1999

Mearns D and Thorn, B [eds], *Person-Centred Therapy Today*, London, Sage Publications, 2000

Milne, A, *Counselling*, London, Hodder and Stoughton, 1999

Norris, D M, T G Gutheil and L H Strasburger, 'This Couldn't happen to Me: Boundary Problems and Sexual Misconduct in the Psychotherapy Relationship', *Psychiatric Services* 54:4 (2003), 517-522

Nye, R D, *Three Psychologies: Perspectives from Freud, Skinner and Rogers*, fourth edition, Belmont, CA, Brooks/Cole, 1992

Owen, I R, 'Boundaries in the Practice of Humanistic Counselling', *British Journal of Guidance and Counselling* 25:2 (1997), 163–174

Padgett, D K, *Qualitative Methods in Social Work Research: Challenges and Rewards*, London, Sage Publications, 1998

Reinharz, S, 'On Becoming a Social Scientist (1979)' in *Practical Social Research,* Hall, D and Hall, I, London, Macmillan, 1996

Robins, C J and Hayes, A M, 'An Appraisal of Cognitive Therapy', *Journal of Consulting and Clinical Psychology* 61 (1993), 205–14

Rogers, C R, 'The Necessary and Sufficient Conditions of Therapeutic Personality Change', *Journal of Consulting Psychology* 21 (1957), 95–103

——, 'The Concept of the Fully Functioning Person', *Psychotherapy: Theory, Research and Practice* 1:1 (1963), 17–26

——, *Client-centred Therapy*, Edinburgh, Constable and Co., 1976

——, *A Way of Being*, Boston, MA, Houghton Mifflin, 1980

Rutter, M, Quinton, D and Liddle, C, 'Parenting in Two Generations: Looking Backwards and Looking Forwards' in *Personality Theory and Clinical Practice,* edited by P Fonagy and A Higgitt, London, Methuen, 1984

Safran, J D, 'Emotion in Cognitive-behavioural Theory and Treatment' in *Trends in Cognitive and Behavioural Therapies*, edited by P M Salkovskis, New York, Wiley, 1996

Salkovskis, P M [ed.], *Trends in Cognitive and Behavioural Therapies*, New York, Wiley, 1996

Scott, M J, Stradling, S G and Dryden, W, *Developing Cognitive-behavioural Counselling*, London, Sage Publications, 1995

Sloane, R B, Staples, F R, Cristol, A H, Yorkson, N J and Whipple, K, 'Short-term Analytical Psychotherapy Versus Behaviour Therapy', *American Journal of Psychiatry* 132 (1975), 373–7

Stringer, E T, *Action Research: a Handbook for Practitioners*, London, Sage Publications, 1996

Swain, J, *The Use of Counselling Skills: A Guide for Therapists*, Oxford, Butterworth-Heinemann, 1995

Tizard, B and Hodges, J, 'The Effect of Early Institutional Rearing on the Development of Eight-year old Children (1978)' in *Personality Theory and Clinical Practice*, edited by P Fonagy and A Higgitt, London, Methuen, 1984

Trower, P, Casey, A and Dryden, W, *Cognitive-behavioural Counselling in Action*, London, Sage Publications, 1988

Warner, M, 'Person-Centred Therapy at the Difficult Edge: A Developmentally Based Model of Fragile and Dissociated Process' in *Person-Centred Therapy Today*, edited by D Mearns and B Thorn, London, Sage Publications, 2000

Webb, S B, 'Training for Maintaining Appropriate Boundaries in Counselling', *British Journal of Guidance and Counselling* 25:2 (1997), 175–188

Wills, F, 'Cognitive Counselling: a Down-to-earth Approach' in *Contracts and Counselling,* edited by C Sills, London, Sage Publications, 1997

Worrall, M, 'Contracting within the Person-Centred Approach' in *Contracts in Counselling,* edited by C Sills, London, Sage Publications, 1997

Yariv, G, 'Blurred Edges', *British Journal of Psychotherapy* 6 (1989), 103–111

Printed in the United Kingdom
by Lightning Source UK Ltd.
123710UK00001B/75/A